Elementary Level
Textbook for Children
Ages 7-9 Years.

Teachings of the Qur'ān

Volume One

Abidullah Ghazi
Tasneema Khatoon Ghazi

IQRA'
International Educational Foundation
Chicago

Part of a Comprehensive and Systematic Program of Islamic Studies

A Textbook for the Program of Qur'anic Studies Elementary Level

Teachings of the Qur'an, Part 1
Second Revised Edition, 1995

Chief Program Editors:
Abidullah al-Ansari Ghazi
Ph.D. History of Religion, Harvard
Tasneema Khatoon Ghazi
Ph.D. Curriculum and Reading, University of Minnesota

Approved by:
Rabita al-Alam al-Islami
Makkah Al-Mukarramah

Reviewers:
Ghulam Haider Aasi
Ph.D. History of Islamic Religion, Temple University
Assad N. Busool
Ph.D. Arabic and Islamic Studies
Irfan Ahmad Khan
Ph.D. Philosophy, University of Illinois
Fadel Abdallah
(M.A. Islamic Studies, University of Minnesota)

Language Editors:
Dr. Khwaja Moinul Hassan
(Ph.D. English Literature, Purdue University)
Noura Durkee
M.A. Fine Arts, Stanford University

Art Direction & Design:
Jennifer Mazzoni
(B.A. Illustration, Columbia College Chicago)

Second Revised Edition, 1995
Third Printing 1997
Fourth Printing 1999
Fifth Printing 2000
Sixth Printing 2004
Seventh Printing 2006
Stamford Press Pte Ltd, Singapore

Library of Congress Catalog Card Number 95-76090
ISBN # 1-56316-101-X

بِسۡمِ ٱللَّهِ ٱلرَّحۡمَٰنِ ٱلرَّحِيمِ

إِنَّا نَحۡنُ نَزَّلۡنَا ٱلذِّكۡرَ وَإِنَّا لَهُۥ لَحَٰفِظُونَ ٩

We have, without doubt, sent down the Message; and we will assuredly guard it (from corruption).
(Al-Hajar 15:9)

Dedicated to:

The Scribe Ṣaḥābah
of
Rasūlullāh, *Ṣalla Allahu 'alai-hi wa-Sallam*
(May Allah's Peace and Blessings be upon Him.)
who
wrote down the Qur'ān
as it was revealed.

Abu Bakr As-Ṣiddīq
'Alī Ibn Abī Tālib
'Umar Ibn al-Khattāb
'Ubai Ibn Ka'b
'Uthmān Ibn 'Affān
Abu Ayyūb al-Ansāri
Abu Salāmah al-Makhzūmī
Abū Sufyān Ibn Ḥarb
Aban Ibn Abī Sufyān
Al-Arqam Ibn Abī al-Arqam
Abū Rāfi'
Buraidah Ibn al-Ḥuṣaib
Thābit Ibn Qais
Juhaim Ibn al-Ṣalt
Ḥanẕalah Ibn al-Rabī'
Al-Ḥuṣain Ibn Numair
Ḥudhaifah Ibn al-Yaman
Ḥuwaiṭib Ibn 'Abd al-'Azīz
Ḥāṭib Ibn 'Amr
Khālid Ibn al-Walīd
Khālid Ibn Sa'īd Ibn al-'Ās
Khālid Ibn Zaid
Zaid Ibn Thābit
Az-Zubair Ibn al-'Awwām
Sa'īd Ibn al-'Ās
Sa'īd Ibn Sa'īd Ibn al-'Ās
As-Sajl
Sa'd Ibn Abī Waqqās
Sa'īd Ibn Abī Waqqās
Shurahbīl Ibn Hasanah
Talḥah Ibn 'Ubaid Allāh
'Āmir Ibn Fuhairah
'Abd Allāh Ibn al-Arqam
'Abd Allah Ibn Ruwāhah
'Abd Allāh Ibn Zaid
'Abd Allāh Ibn Sa'd Ibn Abi As-Sarḥ
'Abd Allah Ibn 'Abd al-'Asad
'Abd Allah Ibn 'Abd Allah Ibn 'Ubai Ibn Salūl
Al-'Alā' Ibn al-Ḥaḍramī
Al-'Ala' Ibn 'Uqbah
'Amr Ibn al-'Ās
Muhammad Ibn Maslamah
Mu'ādh Ibn Jabal
Mu'āwiyah Ibn Abī Sufyān
Mu'aiqib Ibn Abī Fātimah
Al-Muqhīrah Ibn Shu'bah
Yazīd Ibn Abī Sufyān

Riḍwān ullāh 'alai-him 'Ajma'īn
(May Allah be pleased with them all.)

We gratefully acknowledge Dr. Assad N. Busool for this information.

TO PARENTS AND TEACHERS
(Read before you teach this textbook.)

All praises are due to Allah ﷻ and choicest blessing be on Muḥammad, *Ṣalla Allāhu 'alaihi wa-Sallam,* the final messenger who came with the final revelation, the Qur'ān, a light and a guidance for all humankind.

IQRA' International Educational Foundation is grateful to Allah ﷻ for enabling it to do this unique work Teachings of the Qur'ān (Volumes I, II, & III) textbooks of Qur'ānic Studies at elementary level. This is an attempt which is both unique in its presentation and thorough in its application. The three textbooks represent years of hard work in research and application of modern methodology to present the teachings of the Qur'ān to young children.

Teachings of The Qur'ān, in three volumes, introduces young children to the entire range of the message of the Qur'ān at their level of understanding. The authors apply the same, well-tested methodology which has given their *Sīrah* Program (at elementary, junior and senior levels) a great success and acclaim worldwide. The *Sīrah* Program is in use in Islamic schools in the U.S.A. and in most English speaking countries. It has also been translated in several languages.

Teachings of the Qur'ān (I, II, III), along with companion volume Short Sūrahs, represent the first systematic attempt to introduce the message of the Qur'ān to elementary age children at their own level of comprehension and understanding.

IQRA's Comprehensive Program of Qur'ānic Studies, like the Program of *Sīrah,* is produced at four levels and is under final editing and publication. The following points regarding these textbooks should be specially noted by the readers:

- These books are a part of IQRA'S Comprehensive and Systematic Program of Islamic Studies at four levels; Preschool, Elementary, Junior and Senior. More than fifty scholars, educators and professionals are busy in producing this program. So far over sixty-five books are produced. The complete program is expected to have over three hundred books; it will, *Insha'Allah,* be the most comprehensive library of Islamic books and educational material for our children and youth. We expect its completion within the next five years, *Insha' Allah.*

- This volume I, is now completely revised incorporating some very valuable suggestions from teachers and scholars. It is divided into three sections and it deals with the teaching of the Qur'ān on: Islam, the Qur'ān, the *'Imān* and the *'Arkān* (Five Pillars).

- The vocabulary of the *'Āyah,* now added to this volume, is provided at the end of the book as an appendix to help those students who want to pursue further study of the Qur'ān through translation. Such an exercise would greatly help both understanding the Qur'ān and learning Arabic. These books are also an integral Part of Iqra's comprehensive program of Arabic studies which aims to systematically teach Arabic as a second language from an early age.

- Each lesson starts with an *'Āyah,* which is selected to give the message of the Qur'ān on that subject. The *'Āyah* is written both in Arabic and transliterated in English to help the child with the correct pronunciation. The meaning of the *'Āyah* is provided in simple language.

- The message of the *'Āyah* is then explained in short simple sentences. The explanation covers not only the selected *'Āyah* but the general theme of the Qur'ān on that subject the basic message is repeated in three short sentences for reinforcement under: WE HAVE LEARNED.

- A list of new and difficult words is given at the end of each lesson under: DO WE KNOW THESE WORDS.

- A glossary of the words is provided at the end of the book. Workbooks based on the pattern of *Sīrah* program are under publication to provide reinforcement, practice and feedback.

- Iqra' International's efforts in the field of Islamic studies are unique, systematic and comprehensive. Very soon, we hope, the *'Ummah* will realize its full importance and will fully, *Insha'Allah,* benefit from this endeavor. We urge you to join hands and remember us in your *Du'a',* and support this worthy endeavor as *Ṣadaqah Jāriyah* for you and your family.

- IQRA BOOK CLUB membership (at no initial cost and no joining fee) offers your children an opportunity to receive each month a new IQRA' book in your own home to review before paying for it. If you are already our Book Club member, we are sure you appreciate the effort. We request you to introduce the idea to your friends and relatives and you yourself **become our Ansar** and make a commitment to financially support this unique effort.

May Allah ﷻ accept all of our efforts.

Monday 20, June 1994
10 *Muḥarram* 1415

بِسْمِ اللهِ الرَّحْمٰنِ الرَّحِيمِ

Table of Contents

بِسْمِ اللهِ الرَّحْمٰنِ الرَّحِيمِ

IQRA'
TRANSLITERATION CHART

q	ق	*	z	ز		'	أ ء	*
k	ك		s	س		b	ب	
l	ل		sh	ش		t	ت	
m	م		ṣ	ص	*	th	ث	*
n	ن		ḍ	ض	*	j	ج	
h	ه		ṭ	ط	*	ḥ	ح	*
w	و		ẓ	ظ	*	kh	خ	*
y	ي		'	ع	*	d	د	
			gh	غ	*	dh	ذ	*
			f	ف		r	ر	

SHORT VOWELS	LONG VOWELS	DIPHTHONGS
a \ ـَ	a \ ـَا	aw \ ـَوْ
u \ ـُ	u \ ـُو	ai \ ـَيْ
i \ ـِ	i \ ـِي	
Such as: *kataba* كَتَبَ	Such as: *Kitab* كِتَاب	Such as: *Lawḥ* لَوْح
Such as: *Qul* قُلْ	Such as: *Mamnun* مَمْنُون	Such as: *'Ain* عَيْن
Such as: *Ni'mah* نِعْمَة	Such as: *Dīn* دِين	

* Special attention should be given to the symbols marked with stars for they have no equivalent in the English sounds .

ISLAMIC INVOCATIONS:

Rasūlullāh, *Ṣalla Allahu ʻalaihi wa Sallam* (صَلَّى اَللّٰهُ عَلَيْهِ وَسَلَّم), and the Qur'ān teach us to glorify Allāh ﷻ when we mention His Name and to invoke His Blessings when we mention the names of His Angels, Messengers, the *Ṣaḥābah* and the Pious Ancestors.

When we mention the Name of Allāh we must say: *Subḥāna-hū Wa-Taʻālā* (سُبْحَانَهُ وَتَعَالَى), Glorified is He and High.

When we mention the name of Rasūlullāh ﷺ we must say: *Ṣalla Allāhu ʻalai-hi wa-Sallam,* (صَلَّى اَللّٰهُ عَلَيْهِ وَسَلَّم), May Allāh's Blessings and Peace be upon him.

When we mention the name of an angel or a prophet we must say: *Alai-hi-(a)s-Salām* (عَلَيْهِ اَلسَّلَام), Upon him be peace.

When we hear the name of the *Ṣaḥābah* we must say:
For more than two, *Raḍiya-(A)llāhu Taʻālā ʻan-hum,* (رَضِيَ اَللّٰهُ تَعَالَى عَنْهُم), May Allāh be pleased with them.
For two of them, *Raḍiya-(A)llāhu Taʻālā ʻan-humā* (رَضِيَ اَللّٰهُ تَعَالَى عَنْهُمَا), May Allāh be pleased with both of them.
For a *Ṣaḥābī*, *Raḍiya-(A)llāhu Taʻālā ʻan-hu* (رَضِيَ اَللّٰهُ تَعَالَى عَنْهُ), May Allāh be pleased with him.
For a *Ṣaḥābiyyah*, *Raḍiya-(A)llāhu Taʻālā ʻan-hā* (رَضِيَ اَللّٰهُ تَعَالَى عَنْهَا), May Allāh be pleased with her.

When we hear the name of the Pious Ancestor *(As-Salaf as-Ṣāliḥ)* we must say
For a man, *Raḥmatu-(A)llāh ʻalai-hi* (رَحْمَةُ اَللّٰهِ عَلَيْهِ), May Allāh's Mercy be upon him.
For a woman, *Raḥmatu-(A)llāh ʻalai-hā* (رَحْمَةُ اَللّٰهِ عَلَيْهَا), May Allāh's Mercy be with her.

Section I

An Introduction

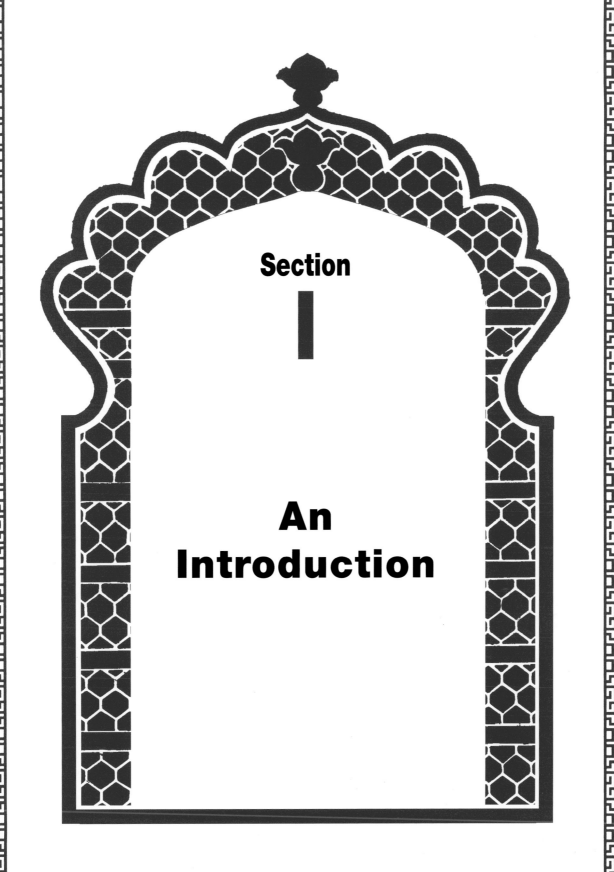

Lesson 1

An Introduction

بِسْمِ اللّٰهِ الرَّحْمٰنِ الرَّحِيْمِ

This book is written especially for you. Through this book we want to teach you the message of the Qur'ān, the most important book for all of humankind. It is a book of guidance for those who seek guidance.

The Qur'ān is *waḥī,* a revelation, from Allah, *Subhanahū wa Ta'āla** to His Prophet Muḥammad, *Ṣallā Allāhu 'alaihi wa Sallam.** It was brought to Prophet Muḥammad ﷺ by angel Jibrīl, *'Alaihi-(a)s–Salām.**

The Qur'ān has one hundred and fourteen chapters. Each chapter of the Qur'ān is called a *Sūrah.* The plural of *Sūrah* is *Suwar.* Each *Sūrah* has several *āyāt* (verses) in it. Some *Suwar* of the Qur'ān are long and some are short.

The Qur'ān is divided in several ways to help people easily read it. It is divided into thirty *'ajzā'*, parts of equal size, and each one of these parts has a name.

Often, we start reading the Qur'ān with the thirtieth *juz'*. This *juz'* has short *Suwar.* Mostly, we read these short *Suwar* in our daily prayers.

We are presenting the Teachings of the Qur'an in three volumes. Each volume contains the teachings of the Qur'an on some important subjects. In these text-books, each lesson starts with an *'āyah,* or part of a long *'āyah,* which explains some important message of the Qur'ān.

* See Islamic Invocations

Each *'āyah* in the lesson is written both in the Arabic and Roman scripts. The meaning of the *'āyah* follows this. Then, each *'āyah* is explained in full detail.

This volume is divided into three parts. Part I deals with the meaning of Islam and the Qur'an. Part II discusses the *'Īmān,* our Islamic faith. The third part covers the *'Arkān,* the five pillars of Islam.

Read each lesson again and again, and try to memorize each *'āyah.* Use the workbook to develop a better understanding of the message of the lesson. Practice what you will learn in each lesson and in this book.

Two Things to Hold Fast

Rasūlullāh ﷺ advised:

"I am leaving you with two things, if you hold fast to them you will not lose your Islamic way ever: They are the Book of Allah (The Qur'an) and my *Sunnah* (way)."

(At-Targhīb wat-Tarhīb)

WE HAVE LEARNED:

* The Qur'ān is sent by Allah ﷻ to Prophet Muḥammad ﷺ through Angel Jibrīl ؑ.
* Qur'ān is divided into *Suwar, ajzā'* and *āyah.*
* We must read each lesson many times, memorize each *'āyah* and practice what we have read.

DO WE KNOW THESE WORDS?

'ajzā'
'āyah
juz'
Sūrah/Suwar
waḥī

Lesson 2

In the Name of Allah ﷻ

بِسْمِ اللّٰهِ الرَّحْمٰنِ الرَّحِيْمِ

Bismillāhi (a)r–Raḥmāni (a)–Raḥīm(i)

"In the name of Allah, Mercy–giving, Merciful."
(An-Naml:27:30 and The Beginning of each *Sūrah* except *Sūrah at–Tawbah)*

EXPLANATION

This is the first *'āyah* (verse) of the Qur'ān. *Ar-Raḥmān* and *Ar-Raḥīm* are two of Allah's Beautiful Names. *Ar-Raḥmān* means the Mercy-giving. *Ar–Raḥīm* means the Merciful. Both of these names show how loving and kind Allah ﷻ is.

Allah ﷻ has ninety nine names. All the names of Allah ﷻ are beautiful.

When we call Allah ﷻ, He hears us. When we ask for Allah's help, He helps us. When we pray to Allah ﷻ, He accepts our prayers.

Every *Sūrah* of the Qur'ān begins with *Bismillāh.* Only *Sūrah at–Tawbah* does not begin with *Bismillāh.* In this *Sūrah* Allah ﷻ shows His anger against the *Mushrikūn* and *Munāfiqūn.*

Mushrikūn are those people who accept partners to Allah ﷻ. *Munāfiqūn* are those people who say they are believers, but in fact, they do not believe.

We must say *Bismillāh* before we begin to read any part of the Qur'ān. We must always say *Bismillāh* before we start to eat our food. We must always say *Bismillāh* before we begin any type of work.

Seek Refuge in Allah ﷾

Allah says in the Qur'ān:

$$\text{فَإِذَا قَرَأْتَ ٱلْقُرْءَانَ فَٱسْتَعِذْ بِٱللَّهِ مِنَ ٱلشَّيْطَنِ ٱلرَّجِيمِ}$$

"When you read the Qur'ān, seek refuge in Allah from *Shaiṭān*, the accursed one."
(An-Naḥl 16:98)

Therefore, when we start reading the Qur'ān, we must say:

$$\text{أَعُوذُ بِاللّٰهِ مِنَ ٱلشَّيْطَنِ ٱلرَّجِيمِ}$$

"A'ūdhu bi-(A)llāhi mina
(a)sh-Shaiṭāni (a)r-Rajīm"
"I seek refuge in Allah from the
Shaiṭān, the accursed one."

Then we must start each reading with *Bismillāh*.

WE HAVE LEARNED:

* *Ar-Raḥmān* and *Ar-Raḥīm* are the two most Beautiful Names of Allah ﷾

* Every *Sūrah*, except *Sūrah at-Tawbah*, begins with *Bismillāh*.

* We must always say *Bismillāh ir-Raḥmān ir-Raḥīm* before we start any work.

DO WE KNOW THESE WORDS?

Mercy-giving
Munāfiqūn
Mushrikūn
Merciful
Ar-Raḥmān
Ar-Raḥīm

بِسْمِ اللّٰهِ الرَّحْمٰنِ الرَّحِيْمِ

اقْرَأْ بِاسْمِ رَبِّكَ الَّذِي خَلَقَ

Iqra' bismi Rabbi ka–(a)lladhī Khalaqa

"Read! In the name of your Lord Who created you"
(Al–'Alaq 96:1)

EXPLANATION

This is the first *waḥī* that Rasūlullāh ﷺ received from Allah ﷻ. The *waḥī* is a message from Allah ﷻ that is sent to His prophets. Angel Jibrīl ؑ brought this *waḥī* to Rasūlullāh ﷺ.

Rasūlullāh ﷺ was in the cave of Ḥirā when Angel Jibrīl ؑ came to him and instructed him to, "Read." Rasūlullāh ﷺ replied, " I do not know how to read." Angel Jibrīl ؑ ordered Rasūlullāh ﷺ again, "Read." Rasūlullāh ﷺ replied again, "I do not know how to read." Angel Jibrīl ؑ then hugged him tightly and asked him to read.

Jibrīl ؑ then recited and Rasūlullāh ﷺ read after him,

> Read! in the name of your Lord, Who created.
> Who created humans from a clot of blood.
> Read! for your Lord is generous.
> Who taught to write with the pen.
> Who taught humankind what it did not know.
> (*Al–'Alaq* 96:1–5)

This was the beginning of Allah's *waḥī* to Rasūlullāh ﷺ. This was the beginning of the Qur'ān. The Qur'ān is

Test 6/15/07

the final *waḥī* of Allah ﷻ. For thirteen years the Qur'ān was revealed to Rasūlullāh ﷺ in Makkah. For the next ten years the Qur'ān was revealed to Rasūlullāh ﷺ in Madīnah. Allah ﷻ did not reveal the Qur'ān all at once, but it was revealed slowly, as the need arose. The entire Qur'ān was revealed in a period of twenty–three years. The first *waḥī* of Allah ﷻ asks all of us to read. It tells us that Allah ﷻ is the only Creator, He created humankind and taught it to read and write.

Allah ﷻ has given us knowledge of the Qur'ān. Allah ﷻ had sent us His last Messenger as a teacher. We must learn the Qur'ān and follow Allah's Messenger.

Reading and Study of the Qur'ān

Rasūlullāh ﷺ told us:
Those people who gather in one of the houses of Allah *(Masjid)* and read the Qur'ān, and discuss its meaning and message, Allah sends upon them peace; His mercy covers them, the angels surround them and Allah remembers them in the company of His angels... (Muslim)

WE HAVE LEARNED:

* The first *waḥī* of Allah ﷻ asks us to read.
* Allah ﷻ taught mankind to read and write.
* We must read the Qur'ān and follow its teachings.

DO WE KNOW THESE WORDS?

'Alaih is–Salām
clot
generous
human
revealed

Lesson 4

The Religion of Islam

Test 2/15/07

بِسْمِ اللَّهِ الرَّحْمَٰنِ الرَّحِيمِ

إِنَّ الدِّينَ عِندَ اللَّهِ الْإِسْلَامُ

Inna-(a)d-dīna ʻind(a) Allāhi-(a)l–Islām

"Surely the true religion with Allah is the Islam."
('Āl ʻImrān 3:19)

EXPLANATION

Islam is the religion of Allah ﷻ. It is the only true religion. Allah ﷻ accepts no other religion besides Islam.

Islam is the first religion of Allah ﷻ. Islam is the religion of all the prophets and the messengers of Allah ﷻ. Islam is the final religion of Allah ﷻ. There will not come a new religion after Islam.

"Islam" comes from the Arabic word *salima*. *Salima* means "to be at peace." From this word, also comes *'aslamah* which means "to obey." Islam, thus, means a "religion of peace." Islam also means a "religion of obedience to Allah ﷻ." Islam teaches that one can only have peace through obeying Allah ﷻ and following His Prophet Muḥammad ﷺ.

Islam teaches us to do those things that Allah ﷻ wants us to do. It teaches us not to do those things that Allah ﷻ does not want us to do.

Islam is the complete religion of Allah ﷻ. Islam is a complete way of life. It teaches us how to lead our lives in this world. It prepares us for the *'Ākhirah*, the life after death. Those who believe in Islam are

Muslims. Muslims are one *'ummah. 'Ummah* means community or nation.

All the Muslims believe that Islam is the religion of Allah ﷻ. All the Muslims believe that the Qur'ān is the last and final Word of Allah ﷻ. All the Muslims believe that Muḥammad ﷺ is the last and final Messenger of Allah ﷻ.

Best *'Ummah*

The Qur'ān tells us about
the Muslim *'ummah:*

كُنتُمْ خَيْرَ أُمَّةٍ أُخْرِجَتْ لِلنَّاسِ تَأْمُرُونَ بِالْمَعْرُوفِ
وَتَنْهَوْنَ عَنِ الْمُنكَرِ

"You are the best *'ummah* (community), that has come out of mankind; you enjoin what is right, you forbid what is wrong..."

('Āl 'Imrān 3:110)

WE HAVE LEARNED:

* Islam is the true and final religion of Allah ﷻ.
* Islam is a religion of peace and obedience to Allah ﷻ.
* Those who believe in Islam are called Muslims, and all Muslims are one *'ummah.*

DO WE KNOW THESE WORDS?

'Ākhirah
'aslamah
Islam
religion
salima
'ummah

بِسْمِ اللهِ الرَّحْمٰنِ الرَّحِيْمِ

ذٰلِكَ الْكِتٰبُ لَا رَيْبَ فِيْهِ هُدًى لِّلْمُتَّقِيْنَ

Dhālika-(a)l–kitābu lā raiba fī–hi, hudal li-(a)l–muttaqīn

"This Book, (the Qur'ān) has no doubts about it at all; it guides to the right path to those who are *Muttaqīn.*"
(Al–Baqarah 2:2)

EXPLANATION

The Qur'ān is Allah's Book. The Qur'ān was brought to Rasūlullāh ﷺ by Angel Jibrīl عليه السلام. The Qur'ān is a *waḥī,* a Revelation. *Waḥī* means direct words of Allah سبحانه وتعالى.

There is no doubt in the teachings of the Qur'ān. The Qur'ān talks about many things that we know and understand. The Qur'ān also teaches us about things that we do not know.

We know about the things that we see, hear, feel and touch. There are many things that we cannot see, hear, feel or touch. Allah سبحانه وتعالى tells us through His *waḥī* about those things that we do not know or cannot know.

Everything that is in the Qur'ān is the Truth. It is a book of guidance for all people.

However, not everyone can benefit from its teachings. Allah سبحانه وتعالى says only a *Muttaqī,* a righteous person, can benefit from the teachings of the Qur'ān. *Muttaqīn* are those who do everything to please Allah سبحانه وتعالى. *Muttaqīn* are those who do not do anything that Allah سبحانه وتعالى dislikes.

Muttaqīn are righteous people who always do things rightly and correctly.

Muttaqīn are those who believe in whatever the Qur'ān teaches about this world and about the *'Ākhirah*, the Hereafter. *Muttaqīn* are those who offer the *Ṣalāh* regularly, give the *Zākah*, and help others for the sake of Allah ﷻ. *Muttaqīn* are successful in this world and in the *'Ākhirah*.

Believing in the Qur'an

Rasūlullāh ﷺ explained to us what believing in the Qur'ān means:

"Allah has enjoined some obligations: don't disobey them; He has forbidden some things: do not do them; He has set some boundaries: do not cross over them; He has not discussed some things: without forgetting them, don't go after them.

(Mishkāt)

WE HAVE LEARNED:

* The Qur'ān is the book of Allah ﷻ sent to Rasūlullāh ﷺ.

* The Qur'ān has no doubts in it.

* The Qur'ān gives guidance to those who are *Muttaqīn*.

DO WE KNOW THESE WORDS?

The *'Ākhirah*
muttaqī
muttaqīn
The *Ṣalāh*
The *Zākah*

بِسْمِ اللهِ الرَّحْمٰنِ الرَّحِيْمِ

وَلَقَدْ يَسَّرْنَا الْقُرْءَانَ لِلذِّكْرِ فَهَلْ مِن مُّدَّكِرٍ

Wa laqad yassarna-(a)l–Qur'āna li-(a)dh–dhikri
fa hal min muddakir

"And indeed! We have made the Qur'ān easy to understand and remember;
but is there any person to do so?"
(Al–Qamar 54:17)

EXPLANATION

The Qur'ān is a miracle of Allah ﷻ. A miracle is something no one can perform except Allah ﷻ. No one can ever write a book like the Qur'ān. Allah ﷻ has made the Qur'ān easy for us to understand and memorize.

The Qur'ān is written in Arabic. The Qur'ān is written in a beautiful style. No one can write in such a beautiful style. The message of the Qur'ān is pure. No human being can write a message as pure as the message of the Qur'ān.

The Qur'ān is the Book of Guidance. It guided the early Muslims. They became the leaders of the world. We must understand the Qur'ān and make it our guide. One who makes the Qur'ān his guide becomes successful in this world and in the Hereafter.

The Qur'ān is easy to memorize. Even those who do not speak Arabic are able to memorize the whole Qur'ān. One who memorizes the entire Qur'ān is called a *ḥāfiẓ*. Throughout the world, there are thousands of *ḥuffāẓ*. Almost every Muslim knows some parts of the Qur'ān by heart.

Allah ﷻ helps those who want to memorize the Qur'ān. Allah ﷻ gives understanding of the Qur'ān to those who try to understand it.

Teaching the Qur'ān

Rasūlullāh ﷺ advised us:

The best among you are those who learn the Qur'ān and teach it to others.

(Ṣaḥīḥ. Al-Bukharī)

WE HAVE LEARNED:

* Allah ﷻ has made it easy for us to memorize the Qur'ān.
* Allah ﷻ has made it easy for us to understand the Qur'ān.
* We should try to memorize and understand the Qur'ān.

DO WE KNOW THESE WORDS?

guidance
ḥāfiẓ
ḥuffāẓ
memorize
miracle

Lesson 7

Read the Qur'ān

بِسْمِ اللهِ الرَّحْمٰنِ الرَّحِيْمِ

فَاقْرَءُوْا مَا تَيَسَّرَ مِنَ الْقُرْءَانِ

Faqra' ū mā tayassara mina-(a)l–Qur' ān(i)

"Read, therefore, of the Qur'ān as much as may be easy for you (to read)."

(Al–Muzzammil 73:20)

EXPLANATION

The Qur'ān is the message of Allah ﷻ. The Qur'ān has been sent for all humankind. The Qur'ān teaches us how to lead a good life in this world. It teaches us how to be successful in the Hereafter.

The Qur'ān guides us to the right path of Islam. It saves us from the wrong path of *kufr*. It also saves us from the wrong path of *shirk*.

We must learn to read the Qur'ān. We must try to memorize the Qur'ān. We should at least try to memorize some parts of the Qur'ān.

We must learn to understand the Qur'ān. We must follow the teachings of the Qur'ān. The Qur'ān is a guide for our life.

We must teach the Qur'ān to others. We must recite the Qur'ān every day. We must read the Qur'ān, as much as we can easily read.

The Qur'ān is the word of Allah ﷻ. It gives us *barakah* in our lives. *Barakah* is the blessing which comes from Allah ﷻ.

Rasūlullāh ﷺ once said to his *Ṣaḥābah:*
"The heart gets rusted as does the iron."

Ṣaḥābah asked him:
"How can we clean the rust of the heart? O Messenger of Allah."

Rasūlullāh ﷺ replied:
"The rust of the heart is cleaned by remembering the death and reading the Qur'ān."

(Mishkāt)

Listen to the Qur'ān

Allah ﷻ says in the Qur'ān:

وَإِذَا قُرِئَ ٱلْقُرْءَانُ فَٱسْتَمِعُوا۟ لَهُۥ وَأَنصِتُوا۟

"When the Qur'ān is recited, listen to it with attention and remain quiet."

(Al-'A'rāf 7:204)

WE HAVE LEARNED:

* The Qur'ān must be recited every day.
* We must read as much of the Qur'ān as is easy for us to read.
* Reading the Qur'ān gives *barakah* to our lives.

DO WE KNOW THESE WORDS?

Barakah
kufr
recite
recitation
shirk

Lesson 8

How to Read the Qur'ān

بِسْمِ اللهِ الرَّحْمٰنِ الرَّحِيْمِ

وَرَتِّلِ ٱلْقُرْءَانَ تَرْتِيلًا

Wa rattili-ﷷl–Qur'ānā tartīlā(n)
"And recite the Qur'ān in *Tartīl*

(slow, measured tones)."
(Al–Muzzammil 73:4)

EXPLANATION

The Qur'ān is the word of Allah ﷻ. Allah ﷻ has sent it through Angel Jibrīl ﷷ. Allah ﷻ has sent it to Rasūlullāh ﷺ.

Angel Jibrīl ﷷ taught Rasūlullāh ﷺ how to recite the Qur'ān. Rasūlullāh ﷺ taught the recitation of the Qur'ān to his *Ṣaḥābaḥ*. The *Ṣaḥābaḥ* taught the recitation of the Qur'ān to those who came after them.

Many people learned the recitation of the Qur'ān. They taught the recitation of the Qur'ān to others. And this is the way we have learned the recitation of the Qur'ān. We have learned to recite the Qur'ān as Rasūlullāh ﷺ taught his *Ṣaḥābaḥ* to recite.

Rasūlullāh ﷺ advised us,
"Recite the Qur'ān in the most beautiful manner."

The art of reciting the Qur'ān is called *tartīl* and *tajwīd*. A person who knows *tartīl* and *tajwīd* is called a *muqri'* or *qārī*.

We must learn how to recite the Qur'ān slowly with *tajwīd*. We must recite the Qur'ān as much as possible. We must recite the Qur'ān as well as possible.

Rasūlullāh ﷺ advises his *Ṣaḥābah:*

"Read the Qur'ān day and night with correct pronunciation, teach its reading to others, recite it in beautiful *tajwīd* and reflect on its meanings, that you may succeed."

Recitation of the Qur'ān

'Umm al-Mu'minīn 'Umm Salma, ؓ was asked about the recitation of Rasūlullāh ﷺ.

She described:
"It was clear and distinct in every letter."

(Ibn Ḥajar; Ibn 'Abd al-Barr)

WE HAVE LEARNED:

* The Qur'ān must be recited in a slow, measured tone.
* The Qur'ān must be recited with *tartīl* or *tajwīd.*
* We must recite the Qur'ān in the best manner possible.

DO WE KNOW THESE WORDS?

Measured
muqri'
qāri'
tajwīd
tartīl

Section II

'Īmān

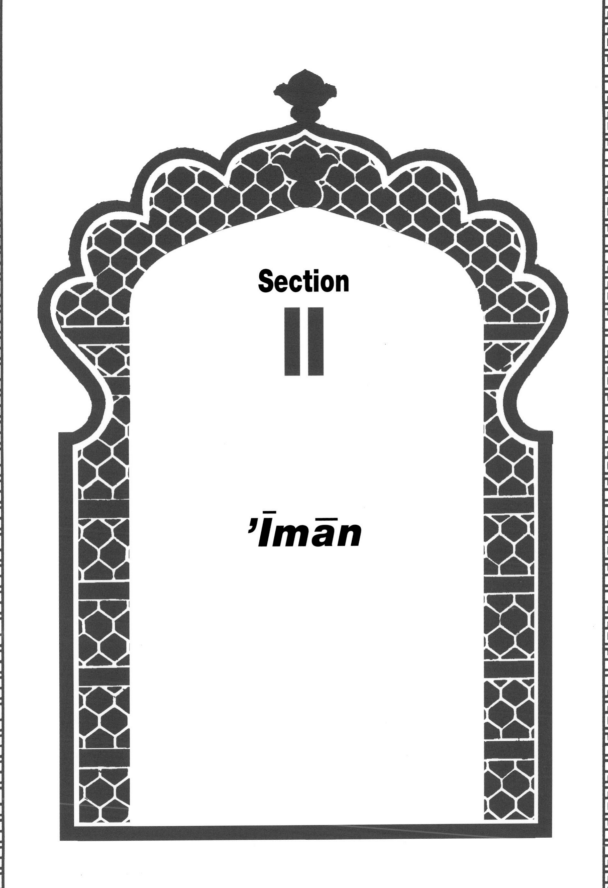

Lesson 9 'Īmān

بِسْمِ اللهِ الرَّحْمٰنِ الرَّحِيْمِ

AN INTRODUCTION

All Muslims have common *'Īmān* (beliefs). Muslims believe in Allah ﷻ, Who is One. Allah ﷻ has no partners, sons or daughters. He has created everyone, and to Him we shall return.

Muslims believe in Allah's messengers. Allah ﷻ sent many prophets and messengers to all the people in the world. All of the messengers brought the same message of Islam. Adam عليه السلام was the first messenger and Muhammad ﷺ is the last.

Muslims believe that Allah ﷻ sent His books to some of the messengers. Most of these books have been changed or are lost. The Qur'ān is the last and final Book of Allah ﷻ. Allah ﷻ, Himself, safeguards this Book.

Muslims believe in the *Malā'ikah,* the Angels. The Angels are made of light. The Angels serve Allah ﷻ and obey His command.

Muslims believe in the *'ākhirah,* the life after death. All those who are born will die one day. Allah ﷻ will judge everyone. Allah ﷻ will reward those who do good deeds. Allah ﷻ will punish those who do evil deeds.

All those who believe in these things are Muslims. All those who do not believe in these things are not Muslims. All those who do not believe in any one of these things, are not Muslims. In the next chapter we shall talk about these beliefs in detail.

Al-'Īmānu-(a)–Muffaṣṣal
The Complete Faith

اَلإِيمانُ الْمُفَصَّلُ

A Muslim must say
with his tongue and believe
with his heart the following:

آمَنْتُ بِاللهِ وَمَلآئِكَتِهِ وَكُتُبِهِ وَرُسُلِهِ

وَالْيَومِ الآخِرِ ،

وَالقَدَرِ خَيْرِهِ وَشَرِّهِ مِنَ اللهِ تَعَالَى

وَالْبَعْثِ بَعْدَ الْمَوتِ .

I believe in Allah, and in His angels, and in His books, and in His messengers and in the *Qadar* (Allah's decree whatever good or bad is in it), and in the rising after death.

WE HAVE LEARNED:

* All Muslims have common beliefs.

* Muslims believe in Allah ﷻ, His Messengers, His Books, His Angels, and in the *'ākhirah*.

* Those who do not believe in these things are not Muslim.

DO WE KNOW THESE WORDS?

The *'ākhirah*
beliefs
command
judge
obey
Qadar

Lesson 10

Blessings of Allah

بِسْمِ اللهِ الرَّحْمٰنِ الرَّحِيْمِ

وَإِن تَعُدُّوا نِعْمَتَ اللَّهِ لَا تُحْصُوهَا

Wa in ta'uddū ni'amat(a)-Allāhi lā tuḥṣū–hā

"And if you would count the blessings of Allah,
you cannot count them."
('Ibrāhīm 14:34)

EXPLANATION

Allah is One, no one shares His Power. Allah has created everything. Everything Allah has created is for the benefit of human beings. No one can ever count the Blessings of Allah.

Allah has given us fresh air to breathe. Allah has given us fresh water to drink. Allah has given us healthy food to eat.

Allah has made us human beings, the best of His creations. Allah has given us the most beautiful forms. Allah has given us brains to think. Allah has given us the power to choose between good and bad. Allah has given us parents, teachers, relatives and friends.

Allah has made us Muslims. He has sent Rasūlullāh ﷺ as His last Messenger. He has made Muslims an *'Ummah* of Rasūlullāh ﷺ.

He has sent His *waḥī,* the Qur'an to guide us. Everything we have is through His Mercy. Everything we do is through His Kindness.

We must always thank Allah for His Blessings. We cannot praise Allah enough for His Kindness. We cannot thank Allah enough for His Mercy. We must thank Allah for the gift of Islam. We must thank Allah for the Message of the Qur'ān. We must thank Allah for the final Prophet Muhammad.

Be Thankful

The Qur'ān reminds us of the many favors of Allah.

وَٱللَّهُ أَخْرَجَكُم مِّنۢ بُطُونِ أُمَّهَٰتِكُمْ
لَا تَعْلَمُونَ شَيْـًٔا
وَجَعَلَ لَكُمُ
ٱلسَّمْعَ وَٱلْأَبْصَٰرَ وَٱلْأَفْـِٔدَةَ ۙ
لَعَلَّكُمْ تَشْكُرُونَ

"And Allah brought you out from the wombs of your mothers,
when you did not know anything;
"And He (Allah) has created for you ears and eyes and hearts
that you be thankful to Him."

(An-Naḥl 16:78)

WE HAVE LEARNED:

* Allah has blessed us with many things.
* No one can ever count the blessings of Allah.
* We must be thankful to Allah for all of His blessings.

DO WE KNOW THESE WORDS?

Benefit
blessing
final
waḥī

Lesson 11

The Will of Allah سبحانه وتعالى

بِسْمِ اللَّهِ الرَّحْمَٰنِ الرَّحِيمِ

وَمَا تَشَاءُونَ إِلَّا أَن يَشَاءَ اللَّهُ رَبُّ الْعَالَمِينَ

We must always ask Allah سبحانه وتعالى for His Blessings.

Wa mā tashā' ūna illā an yashā'
'Allāhu Rabbu (a)–'Ālamīn

"And you do not will unless
Allah, the Lord of the Worlds wills."
(At–Takwīr 81:29)

EXPLANATION

Whatever we have and whatever we get is due to Allah's Mercy. When a Muslim wants to do something, or wishes to get something, he says, *"'Inshā' Allāh."*

'Inshā' 'Allāh means "if Allah is willing." As Muslims we know that we can only do things if Allah سبحانه وتعالى wills them.

Allah سبحانه وتعالى is *Al–'Alīm,* All knowing; He knows what is best for us. Allah سبحانه وتعالى is *Al–Ḥakīm,* All Wise; He does what is best for us. Allah سبحانه وتعالى is *Al–Qawī,* All–Powerful; He has the power to do whatever He wants to do.

Allah سبحانه وتعالى knows what is best for us. He has power to take care of everyone and everything. We cannot do anything without Allah's Permission.

We must always remember Allah سبحانه وتعالى and ask for His Help. When we plan to do something, we should always say *'Inshā' Allāh,* "If Allah is willing." If we get what we want, we should thank Allah سبحانه وتعالى. We must say, *Al–Ḥamdu li–(a)llāh,* "All praises are for

Allah." When we like something, we must say *Subḥān(a) Allāh,* "Glorified is Allah."

When we appreciate something, we must say, *Mā shā' Allāh,* "Whatever Allah wills." If we lose, something or somebody passes away, we must say, *Innā li–(a)llāhi wa 'innā ilaihi rāji'ūn,* "Indeed we belong to Allah سبحانه وتعالى and to Him is our return."

It is Allah's Will

The Qur'ān says Allah's
Will is Final:

قُلِ ٱللَّهُمَّ مَٰلِكَ ٱلْمُلْكِ تُؤْتِى ٱلْمُلْكَ
مَن تَشَآءُ وَتَنزِعُ ٱلْمُلْكَ مِمَّن
تَشَآءُ وَتُعِزُّ مَن تَشَآءُ وَتُذِلُّ
مَن تَشَآءُ بِيَدِكَ ٱلْخَيْرُ إِنَّكَ عَلَىٰ كُلِّ شَىْءٍ قَدِيرٌ

"Say: O Allah! Owner of All-Power, You give Power to whom You Will, and You take away Power from whom You Will; You give honor to whom You Will, and You make low whom You Will; In Your Hand is all the Good. Indeed over everything Thou have Power."

('Āl 'Imran 3:26)

WE HAVE LEARNED:

* We cannot get anything without Allah's Will.
* When we want to do something we should always say *Inshā' Allah.*
* A Believer always trusts the Will of Allah سبحانه وتعالى and remembers Him.

DO WE KNOW THESE WORDS?

Al–'Alīm
Al–Ḥakīm
Al–Qawī
Al–Ḥamdu li–(A)llāh
Innā li–(a)llāhi wa 'innā ilai-hi rāji'ūn
'Inshā' Allāh
Mā shā' Allāh
Subḥan Allāh

Lesson 12

The Help of Allah ﷻ

بِسْمِ اللهِ الرَّحْمٰنِ الرَّحِيْمِ

إِن يَنصُرْكُمُ ٱللَّهُ فَلَا غَالِبَ لَكُمْ

وَإِن يَخْذُلْكُمْ فَمَن ذَا ٱلَّذِى يَنصُرُكُم مِّنۢ بَعْدِهِۦ ۗ

In yansur-kumu-(a)llāhu fā lā ghāliba la-kum,
wa 'in yakhzul–kum fa-man dha-(a)lladhī
yanṣuru–kum min ba'di–hī

"If Allah helps you, no one can defeat you;
if He does not help you, who is there after that,
that can help you."
('Āl 'Imrān 3:160)

EXPLANATION

All power belongs to Allah ﷻ, and no one shares His Power. A Muslim worships Allah ﷻ alone. He always asks Allah ﷻ to help him.

He knows that if Allah ﷻ helps him no one can harm him. If Allah ﷻ does not help him, no one can help him. Someone may help another person only if Allah ﷻ lets him.

This does not mean that a Muslim cannot seek someone's help. A Muslim can ask help from others. He knows that Allah ﷻ, many times, helps us through others. No one can help us without Allah's help. Allah ﷻ always helps those who have trust in Him.

Allah ﷻ also wants us to work hard for whatever we want in life. Trusting in Allah ﷻ means first working hard and then trusting in Him. Allah ﷻ rewards us for our efforts when we work hard and trust in Him.

If a Muslim does not get the things he wants, he should not become angry. If a Muslim is in difficulty, he should not give up hope. He says, "I know that Allah ﷾ loves me and whatever He does is the best for me."

Sometimes we need something; and we try for it, but do not get it. We know Allah ﷾ has something better for us. As Muslims, we trust Allah ﷾ and we seek His help.

Wa Naḥnu 'aqrabu 'ilai–hi min ḥabli (a)–warīd(i)

Allah's Help is Near

Allah ﷾ promises the Believers:

أَلَآ إِنَّ نَصْرَ ٱللَّهِ قَرِيبٌ

"Indeed! the help of Allah is (always) near."

(Al-Baqarah 2:214)

WE HAVE LEARNED:

* When Allah ﷾ decides to help us no one can stop it.
* A Muslim trusts Allah ﷾ and never gives up hope.
* Allah ﷾ always helps those who help themselves.

DO WE KNOW THESE WORDS?

defeat
permission
trust
will

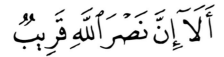

Lesson 13

Allah ﷻ is Near

بِسْمِ اللهِ الرَّحْمٰنِ الرَّحِيْمِ

وَنَحْنُ أَقْرَبُ إِلَيْهِ مِنْ حَبْلِ ٱلْوَرِيدِ

"And We (Allah) are nearer to him
than his jugular vein."
(Qāf 50:16)

EXPLANATION

Allah ﷻ is present everywhere. We do not see Allah ﷻ, but Allah ﷻ sees us all the time. He is closer to us than our jugular vein. This means He is closer to us than we are to ourselves.

Allah is *Al–'Alīm,* All–Knowing and *al–Baṣīr,* All-Seeing. He has created us and has given us everything we have. He knows everything and He sees everything.

He loves and cares for us. When we call Allah ﷻ, He answers our calls. We do not hear His answers, but He accepts our prayers.

The jugular vein carries blood from the heart to the brain. It is the most important vein in the entire body. Allah ﷻ says that He is closer to us than our jug-ular vein. Allah ﷻ means that He is always there to help us.

We should worship Allah ﷻ alone. We should always seek Allah's help. Allah ﷻ hears us and answers our prayers.

Allah ﷻ is our Lord and He is always very close to

us. He always hears our calls and helps us. We should never do *shirk* or *kufr* against Allah سبحانه وتعالى.

Mercy of Allah is Near

Allah سبحانه وتعالى promises in the Qur'an:

إِنَّ رَحْمَتَ ٱللَّهِ قَرِيبٌ مِّنَ ٱلْمُحْسِنِينَ

"Indeed the Mercy of Allah is always near those who do good."

(Al-'A'rāf 7:56)

The Tawbah

وَهُوَ ٱلَّذِى يَقْبَلُ ٱلتَّوْبَةَ
عَنْ عِبَادِهِۦ وَيَعْفُوا۟ عَنِ ٱلسَّيِّـَٔاتِ
وَيَعْلَمُ مَا تَفْعَلُونَ

"He is the One who accepts *tawbah* (repentance) from His servants, and forgives sins and He knows all that you do.

(Ash-Shūrā 42:25)

WE HAVE LEARNED:

* Allah سبحانه وتعالى is even closer to us than we are to ourselves.
* Allah سبحانه وتعالى is kind to us and hears us when we call Him.
* We should never do *kufr* and shirk against Allah سبحانه وتعالى.

DO WE KNOW THESE WORDS?

All–Knowing
All–Seeing
Al–Baṣīr
jugular vein
repentence
tawbah

Lesson 14

Shirk: The Greatest Sin

بِسْمِ اللّٰهِ الرَّحْمٰنِ الرَّحِيْمِ

وَمَن يُشْرِكْ بِٱللَّهِ فَقَدِ ٱفْتَرَىٰٓ إِثْمًا عَظِيمًا

Wa man yushrik bi-(a)llāhi faqad iftarā 'ithman 'azīmā

"Whoever accepts partners with Allah, he has indeed invented a great sin."
(An-Nisā' 4:48)

EXPLANATION

Allah ﷻ is one and no one has any power besides Him. The *Shirk* is the greatest sin in Islam. The *Shirk* means to accept partners to Allah ﷻ. The *Shirk* is to believe that there are other powers besides Allah ﷻ. The *Shirk* is to believe that there is more than one God.

One who does the *Shirk* is called a *Mushrik*. Those who do the *Shirk* are called *Mushrikūn*.

Some people believe that idols are partners with Allah ﷻ. Some people believe that other people share Allah's powers. Some people believe that Angels and Jinns have powers like Allah ﷻ.

Some people believe that the sun, the moon, the stars, the rivers, the animals, the trees and the stones are partners with Allah ﷻ. All these ideas are not right.

All of these ideas are the *Shirk*. The *Shirk* is the worst sin in Islam. Allah ﷻ will forgive all sins, but He will not forgive the *Shirk*.

The example of a *Mushrik* is like a spider who builds a web. “The weakest house,” says the Qur’ān, “is the house of a spider.” *(Al–‘Ankabūt 29:41)*

All of these idols that the *Mushrikūn* worship are helpless.

> “If a fly took something from them, they could not get it back.” *(Al–Ḥajj 22:73)*

Glorified is Allah سبحانه وتعالى; He has no partners and no one is like Him.

Weakness of *Shirk*

Allah gives us an example of the faith of a *Mushrik:*

إِنَّ ٱلَّذِينَ تَدْعُونَ مِن دُونِ ٱللَّهِ
لَن يَخْلُقُوا۟ ذُبَابًا وَلَوِ ٱجْتَمَعُوا۟ لَهُۥ ۖ
وَإِن يَسْلُبْهُمُ ٱلذُّبَابُ شَيْـًٔا لَّا يَسْتَنقِذُوهُ مِنْهُ ۚ

Indeed those on whom you call besides Allah cannot create (even) a fly if they all work together for that purpose. And if the fly took something from them they could not take it back from the fly.
(Al-Ḥajj 22:73)

WE HAVE LEARNED:

* *Shirk* is to believe in any power besides Alla سبحانه وتعالى.
* *Shirk* is the worst sin in Islam.
* Muslims believe in Allah سبحانه وتعالى and worship Him alone.

DO WE KNOW THESE WORDS?

Mushrik
Mushrikūn
power
Shirk

Lesson 15

Kufr: The Worst Sin

بِسْمِ اللهِ الرَّحْمٰنِ الرَّحِيْمِ

إِنَّ شَرَّ ٱلدَّوَآبِّ عِندَ ٱللَّهِ ٱلَّذِينَ كَفَرُوا۟ فَهُمْ لَا يُؤْمِنُونَ

'Inna sharra-(a)–dawābbi 'ind(a)–Allāhi-(a)lladhīna kafarū, fa–hum la yu'minūn(a)

"The worst of beasts in the sight of Allah are those who do *kufr;* indeed they will not believe."
(Al-'Anfāl 8:55)

EXPLANATION

The *Kufr* and the *Shirk* are the two worst sins in Islam. The *Kufr* means to deny Allah ﷻ and to be un-grateful to Him. The *Kufr* also means disbelief in the life after death and in the Day of Judgment.

One who does the *Kufr* is called a *Kāfir*. Those people who disbelieve are called the *Kuffār*. A *Kāfir* is one who denies Allah ﷻ and rejects Him. A *Kāfir* is a disbeliever.

Kufr is like a disease in the hearts of the *Kuffār*. Allah ﷻ seals their hearts because of their *Kufr*. The *Kufr* does not allow them to see the Truth of Allah ﷻ.

Allah ﷻ says in the Qur'ān:

> "Allah is the Protector and Friend of those who believe. He brings them out of darkness and into light. As for those who do *Kufr,* their friends are false idols. They bring them out of light and into darkness." *(Al–Baqarah* 2:257)

Allah ﷻ will protect those who believe and do good deeds.

The *Kuffār* and Their *Kufr*

Allah says in the Qur'ān,

إِنَّ ٱلَّذِينَ كَفَرُوا۟ بَعْدَ إِيمَٰنِهِمْ
ثُمَّ ٱزْدَادُوا۟ كُفْرًا لَّن تُقْبَلَ تَوْبَتُهُمْ

"Those who do *Kufr* after *'Īmān,* and then increase in their *Kufr,* Allah shall never accept their *tawbah* (repentance)"
('Āl 'Imrān 3:90)

وَمَن يَتَبَدَّلِ ٱلْكُفْرَ بِٱلْإِيمَٰنِ
فَقَدْ ضَلَّ سَوَآءَ ٱلسَّبِيلِ

"Whoever exchanges *'Īman* for *Kufr* in fact has gone astray."
(Al-Baqarah 2:108)

WE HAVE LEARNED:

* Allah ﷻ does not like the *Kuffār* and their *Kufr.*
* Muslims believe in *Tawḥīd,* the Oneness of Allah ﷻ.
* Allah ﷻ is going to punish the *Kuffār* for their *Kufr.*

DO WE KNOW THESE WORDS?

'Īman
Kufr
Kāfir
Kuffār

Lesson 16

Messengers of Allah سبحانه وتعالى

بِسْمِ اللَّهِ الرَّحْمَٰنِ الرَّحِيمِ

وَلَقَدْ بَعَثْنَا فِي كُلِّ أُمَّةٍ رَّسُولًا
أَنِ اعْبُدُوا اللَّهَ وَاجْتَنِبُوا الطَّاغُوتَ

Wa laqad ba'athnā fi kulli 'ummatin rasūlan 'ani'budū (a)llāha wa-jtanibū (a)ṭ–ṭāghūta

"And indeed We have sent to every community a messenger (who taught them) to worship Allah and reject the Evil."
(An-Naḥl 16:36)

EXPLANATION

Allah سبحانه وتعالى has sent prophets and messengers to all the people of the world. Angel Jibrīl عليه السلام brought them *Waḥī*. *Waḥī* is the Message of Allah سبحانه وتعالى which came to all the prophets. The Message of all the messengers of Allah سبحانه وتعالى was Islam.

The messengers and prophets invited all of humankind to *Tawḥīd*. They taught people what Allah سبحانه وتعالى wants them to do. They taught people what Allah سبحانه وتعالى does not want them to do. They taught people about the life after death.

There are no people in the world who are left without Allah's Message. There are no people in the world who are left without Allah's messengers and prophets.

The names of only twenty–five prophets are mentioned in the Qur'ān. No one knows the exact number of the prophets that Allah سبحانه وتعالى has sent. Only a few prophets received Allah’s Books.

Those prophets and messengers were human beings. Those prophets and messengers were not gods, nor sons of God. They did not share any power with Allah ﷾. No one shares power with Allah ﷾. The prophets and messengers were servants of Allah ﷾. They taught whatever Allah ﷾ asked them to teach. Adam ﵇ was the first Messenger of Allah ﷾. Muḥammad ﷺ is the last Messenger of Allah ﷾ .

Muslims Believe

قُولُوٓا۟ ءَامَنَّا بِٱللَّهِ وَمَآ أُنزِلَ إِلَيْنَا وَمَآ
أُنزِلَ إِلَىٰٓ إِبْرَٰهِـۧمَ وَإِسْمَـٰعِيلَ وَإِسْحَـٰقَ وَيَعْقُوبَ
وَٱلْأَسْبَاطِ وَمَآ أُوتِىَ مُوسَىٰ وَعِيسَىٰ وَمَآ أُوتِىَ
ٱلنَّبِيُّونَ مِن رَّبِّهِمْ لَا نُفَرِّقُ بَيْنَ
أَحَدٍ مِّنْهُمْ وَنَحْنُ لَهُۥ مُسْلِمُونَ

“Say (O Muslims): We believe in Allah and what is revealed to us that which was revealed to Ibrāhīm, and Ismā‘il, and Isḥāq, and Ya‘qūb, and the tribes, and that which Mūsā and ‘Īsā received, that which the prophets received from their Lord. We make no discrimination between any of them and to Him (Allah) we surrender.”

(Al-Baqarah 2:136)

WE HAVE LEARNED:

* Allah ﷾ has sent His messengers to every people to teach them Islam.

* Messengers are human beings who received Allah’s *Waḥī.*

* All the messengers brought the same Message of Islam.

DO WE KNOW THESE WORDS?

discrimination
messenger
nation
prophet
Waḥī

Lesson

17

The Best Model to Follow

بسم الله الرحمن الرحيم

لَقَدْ كَانَ لَكُمْ فِي رَسُولِ ٱللَّهِ أُسْوَةٌ حَسَنَةٌ

Laqad kāna la-kum fī Rasūli–(a)llāhi
uswatun ḥasanah(tun)

"Indeed! In the Messenger of Allah
you have a good example."
(Al–'Aḥzāb 33:21)

EXPLANATION

Rasūlullāh ﷺ was the last Messenger of Allah سبحانه وتعالى. Allah سبحانه وتعالى sent the Qur'ān to him. The Qur'ān guides us to the Path of Allah سبحانه وتعالى. Rasūlullāh ﷺ practiced what the Qur'ān taught. He showed us how to follow the commands of Allah سبحانه وتعالى. He showed us how to reject the evil plans of the *Shaiṭān.*

Rasūlullāh ﷺ was a Messenger of Allah سبحانه وتعالى. He was a human being. He showed us how to live as family, friends and neighbors. He showed us the best way to lead our lives.

Allah سبحانه وتعالى gave Rasūlullāh ﷺ a most beautiful character. In his life we have the best example to follow. His way and example is called the *Sunnah.* Rasūlullāh's ﷺ *Ṣaḥābah* followed his *Sunnah.* The *Sunnah* is Rasūlullāh's ﷺ teachings and practice.

From the time of Rasūlullāh ﷺ until this time, Muslims have followed his *Sunnah.* The *Sunnah* of Rasūlullāh ﷺ is collected in many books. Rasūlullāh's written *Sunnah* is called the *Ḥadīth.*

Six books of *'Aḥādīth* are very famous. They are

called *Ṣiḥāh Sittah*. *Al–Bukhārī* and *Muslim* are the most important of the *Ḥadīth* books. Rasūlullāh's *Sunnah* is the best example for us to follow.

Allah ﷻ told Rasūlullāh ﷺ in the Qur'ān:

وَإِنَّكَ لَعَلَىٰ خُلُقٍ عَظِيمٍ

You (O Muḥammad) are given
very high morals and manners.
(Al-Qalam 68:4)

The character of Rasūlullāh ﷺ was perfect. His life, teachings and character is the best guide for everyone for all time to come. We must love our Prophet Muḥammad ﷺ. We should follow the *Sunnah* of Rasūlullāh ﷺ.

Obey Rasūlullāh ﷺ

Allah ﷻ has told us:

مَّن يُطِعِ ٱلرَّسُولَ فَقَدۡ أَطَاعَ ٱللَّهَ

"Whoever obeys the Messenger,
indeed obeys Allah."

(An-Nisā' 4:80)

WE HAVE LEARNED:

* In the *Sunnah* of Rasūlullāh ﷺ we have the best example to follow.
* Rasūlullāh's ﷺ *Sunnah* is written in the Books of *'Aḥādith*.
* The six most famous *Ḥadīth* books are called *Ṣiḥāh Sittah*.

DO WE KNOW THESE WORDS?

'Aḥādith
Al–Bukhāri
Muslim
Commands
Ḥadīth
Ṣaḥābah
Ṣiḥāḥ Sittah

Lesson 18

The Example of Rasūlullāh ﷺ

بِسْمِ ٱللَّهِ ٱلرَّحْمَٰنِ ٱلرَّحِيمِ

قُلْ إِن كُنتُمْ تُحِبُّونَ ٱللَّهَ فَٱتَّبِعُونِى يُحْبِبْكُمُ ٱللَّهُ وَيَغْفِرْ لَكُمْ ذُنُوبَكُمْ

Qul 'in kuntum tuḥibbūn(a) Allāha
fattabi'ū–nī yuḥbib–kumu (a)llāhu
wa yaghfir la–kum dhunūba–kum

"Say (to the people O' Muhammad), If you love Allah,
follow me; Allah will love you
and forgive for you your sins."
('Āl 'Imrān 3:31)

EXPLANATION

Allah ﷻ has sent Rasūlullāh ﷺ and made him the best example for us. Allah ﷻ sent Rasūlullāh ﷺ as a mercy to all humankind. Allah ﷻ sent His final Message the Qur'ān, to guide us. Allah ﷻ chose Prophet Muhammad ﷺ as His last Prophet and Messenger.

Allah ﷻ gave him the best morals. Allah ﷻ taught him the best manners. Allah ﷻ gave him the best message.

Rasūlullāh ﷺ worked all his life for Islam. Rasūlullāh ﷺ suffered many hardships for Islam. The *Kuffār* abused him and made fun of him. They stoned him and made him bleed. Finally, Allah ﷻ asked him to leave Makkah.

Rasūlullāh ﷺ showed us how to love Allah ﷻ and serve Him. He taught us that serving Allah ﷻ does not mean giving up this world. He showed us how to worship Allah ﷻ and serve our families, friends and neighbors.

The best way to show our love for Allah ﷾ is to follow the *Sunnah* of Prophet Muḥammad ﷺ.

The Followers of Rasūlullāh ﷺ

وَٱلسَّٰبِقُونَ ٱلْأَوَّلُونَ مِنَ ٱلْمُهَٰجِرِينَ
وَٱلْأَنصَارِ وَٱلَّذِينَ ٱتَّبَعُوهُم بِإِحْسَٰنٍ
رَّضِيَ ٱللَّهُ عَنْهُمْ وَرَضُوا۟ عَنْهُ

The very first of the followers (of Muḥammad) from among the *Muhājirūn* (the immigrants from Makkah), and the *'Anṣār* (the Helpers of Madīnah), and those who follow them in their good deeds; Allah is well-pleased with them, and they are well-pleased with Him.

(At-Tawbah 9:100)

WE HAVE LEARNED:

* We should love Allah ﷾ with all our hearts.
* The *Sunnah* of Rasūlullāh ﷺ shows us how to love Allah ﷾.
* If we follow the *Sunnah* of Rasūlullāh ﷺ Allah ﷾ will love us.

DO WE KNOW THESE WORDS?

'Anṣārs
guide
Manners
Muhājirūn
morals
Sunnah

Lesson

19

صلى الله عليه وسلم

Love of Rasūlullāh

بِسْمِ اللهِ الرَّحْمٰنِ الرَّحِيمِ

ٱلنَّبِيُّ أَوْلَىٰ بِٱلْمُؤْمِنِينَ مِنْ أَنفُسِهِمْ ۖ وَأَزْوَٰجُهُۥٓ أُمَّهَٰتُهُمْ ۗ

An–Nabiyyu 'awlā bi-(a)–Mu'minīna min 'anfusi–him wa-'azwāju–hu 'ummahātu–hum

"The prophet is closer to the Believers than their own selves, and his wives are their mothers"
(Al-'Aḥzāb 33:6)

EXPLANATION

Rasūlullāh ﷺ was a kind and generous person. He helped and cared for everyone. He wanted all people to know Allah's religion, Islam. Those who believe in Rasūlullāh ﷺ and follow him are his *'ummah.*

Rasūlullāh ﷺ loved his *'ummah.* Rasūlullāh ﷺ loved his *'ummah* more than he loved himself. We are the *'ummah* of Rasūlullāh ﷺ and we should love him more than we love ourselves.

We must be ready to sacrifice everything for the sake of Rasūlullāh ﷺ. Rasūlullāh ﷺ is like a father to his *'ummah.* His wives are like mothers to the Believers. His wives are called *'Ummahātu (a)l–Mu'minīn.*

'Ummahātu (a)l–Mu'minīn means the "Mothers of the Believers." Rasūlullāh's ﷺ wives were kind and generous. They helped the poor and the needy.

They supported Rasūlullāh ﷺ in his work for Islam. They were ready to sacrifice everything for the cause of Islam. They are the best example for Muslim women to follow. They are also the best example for all Muslims to follow.

Muslims love Rasūlullāh ﷺ and follow his *Sunnah.* Muslims also love *'Ummahātu (a)l–Muminīn* as their mothers. We show this love by following their examples.

> ## True Love
>
> Rasūlullāh ﷺ advised us:
>
> "Those who are happy with the fact that they love Allah and His Messenger, they should always speak the Truth. When they receive something in trust they must return it to its owner (when demanded by him) and be kind to their neighbors."
>
> *(Mishkāt)*

WE HAVE LEARNED:

* We must love Rasūlullāh ﷺ more than we love ourselves.
* Rasūlullāh's ﷺ wives are *'Ummahātu (a)l–Mu'minīn*, the Mothers of the Believers.
* *'Ummahātu (a)l–Mu'minīn* are the best examples for us to follow.

DO WE KNOW THESE WORDS?

Honor
The Mothers of the Believers
'Ummahātu (a)l–Mu'minīn

Lesson 20

The Books

بِسْمِ اللهِ الرَّحْمٰنِ الرَّحِيمِ

جَآءَتْهُمْ رُسُلُهُم بِٱلْبَيِّنَٰتِ وَبِٱلزُّبُرِ وَبِٱلْكِتَٰبِ ٱلْمُنِيرِ

Jā' at–hum rusulu–hum bi-(a)–bayyināti
wa bi-(a)z–Zuburi wa bil–Kitābi (a)l–munīr(i)

"Their Messengers came to them with clear proofs, and with *Zabūr,* and the Book giving light."
(Fāṭir 35:25)

EXPLANATION

Allah ﷻ has sent many prophets *('Anbiyā')* and messengers *(Rusul)* and guided them with His *waḥī*. He sent His Books through Angel Jibrīl عليه السلام to some of the prophets. The prophets who received His Books are called *Rusul*.

Prophet Ibrāhīm عليه السلام received *Ṣuḥuf,* the Books.
Prophet Mūsā عليه السلام received *At-Tawrāt,* the Torah.
Prophet Dāwūd عليه السلام received *Zabūr,* the Psalms.
Prophet ʿĪsa عليه السلام received *Al-Injīl,* the Gospel. Prophet Muhammad ﷺ received the Qur'ān.

All the Books of Allah ﷻ teach *Tawḥīd*. All the Books tell people that Allah ﷻ is the only God. They tell people not to accept partners with Allah ﷻ.

The Books of Allah ﷻ teach how to lead a good Islamic life. They teach us about our duties to each other. They teach that we should care for each other and be good servants of Allah ﷻ.

Allah's Books teach us about following the laws of Allah ﷻ. Allah's laws ask people to offer the *Ṣalāh,* observe the *Ṣawm,* pay the *Ẓakāh* and perform the *Ḥajj.*

Some of the Books of Allah ﷻ are lost completely. The teachings of some other books have been changed.

The Qur'ān is the last and final Book of Allah ﷻ. Allah ﷻ Himself safeguards this Book. No one will ever be able to change its words or meanings.

Live by the Qur'ān

Once Rasūlullāh ﷺ passed by some of his *Ṣaḥabāh.* He asked them, "Do you believe that there is no god but Allah and I am Allah's Messenger?"

The *Ṣaḥabāh* replied, "Yes, O Rasūlullāh, we do!"

Rasūlullāh then advised them: "One end of this Qur'an is in the hands of Allah and the other end is in your hand; so live by it. Indeed, you shall not go astray, nor shall you be destroyed."

(At-Targhīb wa-(a)t-Tarhīb)

WE HAVE LEARNED:

* Allah ﷻ has sent many Books through His messengers to mankind.
* All these Books guide us to the right path of Islam.
* The Qur'ān is the last and final Book of Allah ﷻ.

DO WE KNOW THESE WORDS?

Al-'Injīl
Rusul
Ṣuḥuf
Safeguards
At-Tawrāt
Az-Zabūr

Lesson 21

The *Malā'ikah:* The Angels

بِسْمِ ٱللَّهِ ٱلرَّحْمَٰنِ ٱلرَّحِيمِ

ٱلْحَمْدُ لِلَّهِ فَاطِرِ ٱلسَّمَٰوَٰتِ وَٱلْأَرْضِ جَاعِلِ ٱلْمَلَٰٓئِكَةِ رُسُلًا

Al-ḥamdu li–Allāhi fāṭiri (a)s–Samāwāti wa-(a)l-'Arḍi Jā'il-(a)l–Malā'ikati rusulā(n)

"Praise be to Allah the Creator of the heavens and the earth, Who sent the *Malā'ikah as* messengers."
(Fāṭir 35:1)

EXPLANATION

Muslims believe in Allah's *Malā'ikah,* the angels. The *Malā'ikah* are creatures of Allah سبحانه وتعالى. The *Malā'ikah* are made of light. We cannot see them, but they see us.

The *Malā'ikah* do whatever Allah سبحانه وتعالى asks them to do. The *Malā'ikah* do not disobey Allah سبحانه وتعالى.
The *Malā'ikah* are not sons or daughters of Allah سبحانه وتعالى.

Malā'ikah are busy doing many jobs all the time. Some *Malā'ikah* protect and help people. Some of them are in charge of *Jannah,* the Paradise. Other *Malā'ikah* are in charge of *Jahannam*, the Hell.

Some *Malā'ikah give* praise to Allah سبحانه وتعالى all the time. We all have two *Malā'ikah* that write down all our good and bad deeds. Angel *Jibrīl* عليه السلام brought Allah's *waḥī* to the Prophets. Angel *'Isrāfīl* عليه السلام will blow *Aṣ-Ṣūr,* a loud trumpet, to begin the Day of Judgment.

Angel *'Izrā'īl* عليه السلام comes to people at the time of death, to take their souls out of their bodies. Angel *Mīkā'īl* sees that we get enough rainfall. Angels are not partners of Allah ﷻ, but are Allah's ﷻ creation and His servants.

The Muslims' Belief

The Qur'ān says:

ءَامَنَ ٱلرَّسُولُ بِمَآ أُنزِلَ إِلَيْهِ
مِن رَّبِّهِۦ وَٱلْمُؤْمِنُونَ كُلٌّ ءَامَنَ بِٱللَّهِ
وَمَلَٰٓئِكَتِهِۦ وَكُتُبِهِۦ وَرُسُلِهِۦ

"The Messenger believes what has been revealed to him from his Lord. So do the Believers believe. Both (the Prophet and the Believers) believe in Allah, His *Malā'ikah,* His Scriptures and His Messengers."

(Al-Baqarah 2:285)

WE HAVE LEARNED:

* The Angels are made of light.

* They are always busy doing Allah's commands.

* We cannot see the Angels, but the Angels see us.

DO WE KNOW THESE WORDS?

disobey
Malā'ikah
Malak
Aṣ-Ṣūr
trumpet

Lesson 22

Al-Ākhirah

بِسْمِ اللهِ الرَّحْمٰنِ الرَّحِيمِ

وَلَدَارُ الْآخِرَةِ خَيْرٌ ۚ وَلَنِعْمَ دَارُ الْمُتَّقِينَ

Wa la-dāru-(a)l-'Ākhirati khairun
wa la-ni'ma
dāru-(a)l-muttaqīn

"And the *'Ākhirah* will be better (than this world).
And pleasant indeed will be
the home of the righteous."
(An–Naḥl 16:30)

EXPLANATION

As Muslims, we believe that our lives in this world are short. There is another life after this life that lasts forever. There is another world after this world.

This world is called *Ad–Dunyā.* The world we go after our death is *Al–'Ākhirah,* the Hereafter. Everyone who is born will die one day. Everyone will be born again in *'Al–'Ākhirah.* Everyone will be judged by Allah ﷻ for his deeds.

Those who believed and did good works will be rewarded with *Jannah.* Those who did not believe and did not do good deeds will be sent to *Jahannam.*

Jannah is the beautiful garden of Heaven. Those who believed and did good deeds will live in *Jannah* for ever. They will be given the most beautiful things. They will have the most beautiful form.

Jahannam is the everlasting fire of Hell. The people of *Jahannam* will be punished for their worng actions. The pleasures of the *'Ākhirah* are much better than the pleasures of this world.

The pleasures of this world are for a short period. The pleasures of the *'Ākhirah* are forever. The pleasures of the *'Ākhirah* are only for the righteous.

Ad-Dunyā and *Al-'Ākhirah*

Allah says in the Qur'ān:

فَمَا مَتَـٰعُ ٱلْحَيَوٰةِ ٱلدُّنْيَا فِى ٱلْـَٔاخِرَةِ إِلَّا قَلِيلٌ

"The comfort of the life of this world *(Ad-Dunyā)* is little, as compared with the Hereafter."

(At-Tawbah 9:38)

WE HAVE LEARNED:

* *Ad–Dunyā,* this world is for a short period of time.
* The life of the *'Ākhirah*, is forever.
* The pleasures of the *'Ākhirah* are for the righteous.

DO WE KNOW THESE WORDS?

Ad–Dunyā/the *Dunya*
Al-'Ākhirah/the *'Ākhirah*
Hereafter
Jannah

Section III

The Five *'Arkān*

Lesson 23

Five *Arkān*: The Five Pillars

بِسْمِ اللّٰهِ الرَّحْمٰنِ الرَّحِيْمِ

AN INTRODUCTION

Just like a building is supported by its pillars, the faith of a Muslim is supported by the five pillars, the *'Arkān* of Islam. The Islamic pillars, however, are not pillars of stone or concrete. They are pillars of belief. The five *'Arkān* of Islam are:

- The *Shahādah,* to believe that there is no god but Allah, and that Muḥammad ﷺ is the Messenger of Allah.
- The *Ṣalah,* to pray five times every day.
- The *Ṣawm,* to fast in the month of *Ṛamaḍān.*
- The *Ẓakāh,* to share one's savings with the poor and needy.
- The *Ḥajj,* to make pilgrimage to Makkah once in the lifetime.

The five *'Arkān* are *farḍ* (obligatory), on every Muslim man and woman. *Farḍ* means that we should believe in them and we should do them. All Muslims must believe in the five *'Arkān* and follow them.

Being born in a Muslim family does not make one a Muslim. Neither does having a Muslim name make one a Muslim. A Muslim is one who believes in the teachings of the Qur'ān and acts on those teachings.

Let us learn about the five *'Arkān* of Islam, as the Qur'ān teaches them. Let us practice them all the time.

'Īmān and 'Islām

Once Rasūlullāh ﷺ was seated among his *Ṣaḥābah* when Angel Jibrīl ﷺ came to Rasūlullāh ﷺ in the form of a human and asked him, "What is 'Īmān?"

Rasūlullāh ﷺ replied, "'Īmān is to believe in Allah, His Angels, and in meeting with Him; and believe in His Messengers, and His Books and in the life after death."
The Angel heard this and said, "You are right O, Muhammad."

Then he asked, "O Muhammad, what is Islam?" Rasūlullāh ﷺ replied, "Islam is to worship only Allah and not to accept partners with Him, establish the *Ṣalāh,* pay the *Zakāh,* observe fast in the month of *Ramaḍān* and perform pilgrimage to Makkah, if one has the resources."
The Angel confirmed, "You are right O Muhammad."

(Al-Bukhārī)

WE HAVE LEARNED:

* The faith of a Muslim is supported by the five *'Arkān* of Islam.
* The five *'Arkān* are *farḍ* on every Muslim.
* All Muslims must believe in the five *'Arkān* and follow them.

DO WE KNOW THESE WORDS?

Farḍ
obligatory
Shahādah
pillar

Lesson 24

Shahadah: Allah ﷻ

بِسْمِ اللهِ الرَّحْمٰنِ الرَّحِيْمِ

فَاعْلَمْ أَنَّهُۥ لَآ إِلٰهَ إِلَّا ٱللَّهُ

Fa-(a)'lam 'anna–hū lā 'ilāha ill(a)–Allāhu

"So, know that, there is no god except Allah."
(Muḥammad 47:19)

EXPLANATION

Allah ﷻ is One. No one is like Him. There is no god besides Him. There is no power except Him.

He has created everyone and everything. No one has created Him. He takes care of everyone and everything. No one takes care of Allah ﷻ. All of us need Allah ﷻ to live. Allah ﷻ does not need anyone to live.

Allah ﷻ is One. He has no partners. He has no father and no mother. He has no daughter and no son.

Some people believe that Allah has partners. Some people believe that Allah ﷻ has a son. Some people believe Allah ﷻ has daughters. Some people believe that Allah ﷻ has a wife and family.

Such beliefs are called the *Shirk*. *The Shirk* is the greatest sin in Islam. Allah ﷻ is the Creator and Lord of everything. Allah ﷻ does not need a son or a daughter or a family.

Some people do not believe in Allah ﷻ. Such an idea is called *Kufr*. The *Kufr* is also a great sin in Islam.

All of these ideas are wrong. Allah ﷻ is glorified; He has no partners. Muslims know that there is no god except Allah ﷻ. Allah ﷻ has created us; He supports us and to Him we shall return.

Perfect Faith

'Amr ibn Wābiṣah ؓ asked Rasūlullāh ﷺ, "What is true faith, O Messenger of Allah?"

Rasūlullāh ﷺ replied, "Whoever loves for the sake of Allah, and hates for the sake of Allah, and spends for the sake of Allah, has in fact perfected his faith."

(Al-Bukhārī)

WE HAVE LEARNED:

* The first part of *Shahādah* is, "There is no god but Allah."

* The Muslims do not believe in *kufr* and *Shirk*.

* *Kufr* and *Shirk* are the worst sins in Islam.

DO WE KNOW THESE WORDS?

partner
support

Lesson 25

Shahādah: The Messenger

بِسْمِ اللّٰهِ الرَّحْمٰنِ الرَّحِيْمِ

مُحَمَّدٌ رَّسُولُ اللّٰهِ

Muḥammadu(n)-r-Rasūlullāh

"Muhammad is the Messenger of Allah."
(Al–Fatḥ 48:29)

EXPLANATION

Allah ﷻ has sent many prophets and messengers. The prophets and messengers were sent to all the people. Allah ﷻ sent them His *Waḥī,* Revelation. The *Waḥī* is Allah's Message to all humankind.

Allah ﷻ chose to give His Books to some of the prophets. A prophet *(Nabī)* who received Allah's Book is called a *Rasūl. Rasūl* means a messenger. *Nabī* means a prophet.

Allah ﷻ sent Muḥammad ﷺ as a prophet and a messenger to humankind. Muḥammad ﷺ is Allah's last *Nabī* to humankind. Muḥammad ﷺ is *Nabī-Allāh.* Muḥammad ﷺ is Allah's last messenger. Muḥammad ﷺ is *Rasūlullāh* ﷺ. Muḥammad ﷺ is Allah's last *Rasūl* and *Nabī.* Muḥammad ﷺ was a human being and a servant of Allah ﷻ. Allah ﷻ sent to Prophet Muḥammad ﷺ His final book the Qur'ān. Allah ﷻ says in the Qur'ān:

> "Indeed Allah and the angels sent salutation on the Prophet, O' Believers, send Salutations and your *Salām* upon him."
> *(Al–'Aḥzāb 33:56)*

When we hear the name of our Prophet Muḥammad ﷺ we must say:

"Ṣall(a)Allāhu 'alai-hi wa Sallam."

That means ,"May Allah's Blessings and Peace be upon him." We write an ﷺ after the name of Rasūlullāh. This reminds us to say *Ṣall(a)Allāhu 'alai-hi wa Sallam.*

The Final Seal

Allah says in the Qur'ān

مَّا كَانَ مُحَمَّدٌ أَبَآ أَحَدٍ مِّن رِّجَالِكُمْ وَلَٰكِن
رَّسُولَ ٱللَّهِ وَخَاتَمَ ٱلنَّبِيِّـۧنَ

Muḥammad is not the father of any one of you, but he is the Messenger of Allah and the Final Seal of the Prophets.

(Al-'Aḥzāb 33:40)

WE HAVE LEARNED:

* The second part of the *Shahādah* is to say that Muḥammad ﷺ is the Messenger of Allah.
* Muḥammad ﷺ is *Nabī-Allāh* and Rasūlullāh.
* When we hear the name of Rasūlullāh we must say, *Ṣall(a)Allāhu 'alaihi wa Sallam.*

DO WE KNOW THESE WORDS?

Salutation
Nabī-Allāh
Rasūlullāh
Ṣall(a)Allāhu 'alai-hi wa Sallam.

بِسْــمِ اللهِ الرَّحْمٰنِ الرَّحِــيْمِ

وَأْمُرْ أَهْلَكَ بِٱلصَّلَوٰةِ وَٱصْطَبِرْ عَلَيْهَا

Wa'mur 'ahla–ka bi-(a)ṣ–Ṣalāti wa–(a)ṣṭabir 'alai–hā

"And enjoin upon your family the *Ṣalāh*
and be regular in it."
(Ṭāhā: 20:132)

EXPLANATION

The *Ṣalāh* is the second pillar of Islam. The five daily prayers are *farḍ*, or an obligation for every Muslim. *Farḍ* means that one is required to do it no matter what. The *Ṣalāh* is the most important *farḍ* for every Muslim.

Rasūlullāh ﷺ said,

> "The first thing people will be asked about on the Day of Judgment is the *Ṣalāh*."

The prophets were asked by Allah ﷻ to enjoin the *Ṣalāh* upon their people. The parents must enjoin the *Ṣalāh* on their children. We should remind each other to offer the *Ṣalāh*.

We should try to offer the *Ṣalāh* with the *jamā'ah*. The *jamā'ah* is a prayer in a group behind an *'imām*. Making *'Adhān* at the time of each *Ṣalāh* is a call to offer *Ṣalāh* with *jama'ah*. Those who make *'Adhān* and *Iqāmah* get a special reward from Allah ﷻ.

One should try to offer the *Ṣalāh* in the *masjid* with the *jama'ah*. If there is no *masjid* in the neighborhood, we must offer the *Ṣalāh* at home with the *jama'ah*. If one cannot offer the *Ṣalāh* with the *jama'ah* then he or she must offer it alone. Even two persons can make a *jama'ah*.

Ṣalāh Safeguards

Allah says in the Qur'ān:

إِنَّ ٱلصَّلَوٰةَ تَنْهَىٰ عَنِ
ٱلْفَحْشَآءِ وَٱلْمُنكَرِ

"Indeed the *Ṣalāh* safeguards from shameful and evil acts."
(Al-'Ankabūt 29:45)

A Clean Person

Rasūlullāh ﷺ once asked his *Ṣaḥabāh,* "If someone took a bath five times a day in the river flowing by his house, would there remain any dirt on his body?"
The *Ṣaḥabāh* replied,
"No dirt will remain on him,
O, Messenger of Allah."

Rasūlullāh ﷺ then said, "Such is the example of one who offers the *Ṣalāh* five times a day. Allah re-moves the dirt of his sins from him."

(Al-Bukhārī, Muslim)

WE HAVE LEARNED:

* One should offer the *Ṣalāh* regularly.
* We should remind others to offer the *Ṣalāh.*
* We must try to offer the *Ṣalāh* with the *jamā'ah.*

DO WE KNOW THESE WORDS?

enjoin
'īqāmah
jamā'ah
judgment
obligation

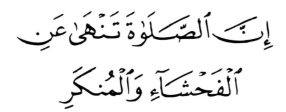

Lesson 27

The Ṣawm: The Fasting

بِسْمِ اللهِ الرَّحْمٰنِ الرَّحِيمِ

يَـٰٓأَيُّهَا ٱلَّذِينَ ءَامَنُوا۟ كُتِبَ عَلَيْكُمُ ٱلصِّيَامُ كَمَا كُتِبَ عَلَى ٱلَّذِينَ مِن قَبْلِكُمْ لَعَلَّكُمْ تَتَّقُونَ

Yā 'ayyuh(a) alladhīna 'āmanu kutiba 'alai–kumu (a)ṣ–Ṣiyāmu kamā kutiba 'ala–(a)lladhīna min qabli–kum la'alla–kum tattaqūn.

"O Believers! *Ṣiyām,* fasting, is made obligatory for you as it was made obligatory for people before you, that you may learn *taqwa* (righteousness)."
(Al-Baqarah 2:183)

EXPLANATION

The *Ṣawm*, fasting, is the third pillar of Islam. It is a *farḍ* (obligation) for every adult Muslim. Muslims must fast in the month of *Ramaḍān*. The *Ṣawm* was made *farḍ* for people before us.

The *Ṣawm* is made *farḍ* for us so that we may learn the *Taqwā.* The *Taqwā* teaches us how to love Allah and obey Him. The *Taqwa* teaches us to be always righteous. The *Ṣawm,* the fast, is a special *'ibādah* to please Allah ﷻ. We fast only for the sake of Allah ﷻ. People who fast are very special to Allah.

The fasting allows us to know how it feels to be hungry. There are many people in the world who do not have enough to eat. The hungry and the needy are in need of our help. We must share with others whatever Allah ﷻ has given us.

Allah ﷻ has made fasting obligatory on us in order to

make us righteous. A ṣawm is to give up food and drink for a day. A true ṣawm is also to give up bad habits for ever. A true ṣawm means we should not fight, lie or use bad language.

The Ṣawm teaches us to be always patient. It teaches us to share the Blessings of Allah ﷻ with others. To gain the pleasure of Allah ﷻ we must be ready to give up those things that we love.

A Ṣawm without giving up bad habits is like going hungry. There is no reward for such a Ṣawm.

Allah's Promise

'Abū Hurairah ؓ related from Rasūlullāh ﷺ, that Rasūlullāh ﷺ said,

"The reward of each good action is from ten to one hundred times with Allah, but the reward of fasting is an exception. Allah promises, 'Fasting is for My sake, and I will give its reward (as much as I want).'"

(Al-Bukhārī, Muslim)

WE HAVE LEARNED:

* The Fasting in the month of *Ramaḍān* is *farḍ* for every Muslim.

* Muslims should fast in the month of *Ramaḍān*.

* The Fasting teaches us to share whatever we have with others.

DO WE KNOW THESE WORDS?

'Ibādah
prevent
Ramaḍān
the ṣawm
the ṣiyām

Lesson 28

The Ẓakāh

بِسْمِ اللهِ الرَّحْمٰنِ الرَّحِيمِ

فَأَقِيمُوا الصَّلَوٰةَ وَءَاتُوا الزَّكَوٰةَ وَاعْتَصِمُوا بِاللَّهِ هُوَ مَوْلَىٰكُمْ

Fa 'aqīmu-(a)ṣ-Ṣalāta wa 'ātu-(a)z-Zakāta w'ataṣimū bi-(a)llāhi Huwa Mawlā–kum

"So offer the *Ṣalāh,* and pay the *Ẓakāh,* and hold fast to Allah; He is your Master."
(Al–Ḥajj 22:78)

EXPLANATION

The *Ẓakāh* is the fourth pillar of Islam. The *Ẓakāh* is mentioned very often in the Qur'ān with the *Ṣalāh.* It shows how important the *Ẓakāh* is. It is a *farḍ,* like the *Ṣalāh* and the *Ṣawm.* The *Ẓakāh* means to purify and make something clean.

The *Ṣalāh* and the *Ṣawm* are *farḍ* for every adult Muslim. The *Ẓakāh* is *farḍ* for only those Muslims who have enough savings. The *Ẓakāh* must be paid by the rich people to the needy and the poor.

The *Ẓakah* teaches us to care about the poor and the needy. It teaches us to share our money and wealth with others. It teaches us to trust Allah ﷻ and to give our money for His pleasure.

Those who pay the *Ẓakāh* to the needy must not expect anything in return from them. They should not even think that they are doing a favor to someone. They should seek their reward only from Allah ﷻ. The *Ẓakāh* is a fixed amount of our savings that we must give in charity. The *Ẓakāh* is a *farḍ* that we must fulfill.

Allah ﷻ wants us to give more than *Zakāh* in His way. Allah ﷻ is happy with us when we give more. Such a giving is called *Ṣadaqah*. Whatever we give in this world, Allah ﷻ saves for us in the *'Ākhirah*.

The reward in the *'Ākhirah* is many times more than what we receive in this world. By offering the *Ṣalāh* and paying the *Zakāh*, we hold fast to Allah ﷻ, our Lord. If we hold fast to Allah ﷻ, no one can hurt us or harm us.

Ṣadaqah

Rasūlullāh ﷺ informed us:

Allah says, "O children of Adam,
you spend (on the needy),
I will spend on you."

(Al-Bukhārī, Muslim)

WE HAVE LEARNED:

* The *Zakāh* is a fixed amount of our savings, that we must give in charity.
* We must pay the *Zakāh* and *Ṣadaqah* to the poor and the needy.
* By offering the *Ṣalāh* and paying the *Zakāh*, we hold fast to Allah ﷻ.

DO WE KNOW THESE WORDS?

Charity
Children of Adam
Ṣadaqah
savings
wealth
Zakāh

Lesson 29

The *Ḥajj*: The Pilgrimage

بِسۡمِ ٱللّٰهِ ٱلرَّحۡمٰنِ ٱلرَّحِيۡمِ

وَلِلَّهِ عَلَى ٱلنَّاسِ حِجُّ ٱلۡبَيۡتِ مَنِ ٱسۡتَطَاعَ إِلَيۡهِ سَبِيلًا

Wa li-(a)llāhi ʻala-(a)n-nāsi ḥijju-(a)l–baita mani-(i)staṭāʻa' ilai–hi sabīlā(n)

"And *Ḥajj* to the House (of Allah) is a duty of people to Allah; but for those who can afford."
('Āl 'Imrān 3:97)

EXPLANATION

The *Ḥajj,* the Pilgrimage, to *Bait–Allāh*, the House of Allah, is the fifth pillar of Islam. The *Ḥajj* is not a *farḍ* for every Muslim. It is *farḍ* only for those who are healthy and for those who have enough money to pay for their *Ḥajj.*

They must be able to support their families while they are gone for the *Ḥajj.* They must perform the *Ḥajj,* at least, once in their lifetime. To perform the *Ḥajj,* people go to *Bait–Allāh* in Makkah.

The *Ḥajj* brings Muslims from all over the world to Makkah. Muslims come from many different countries. There are people of all colors: black, white, yellow and brown. All of them are Believers and all of them are brothers and sisters in Islam. All of them are the *'ummah* of Muḥammad ﷺ. In the *Ḥajj*, Allah سُبۡحَانَهُ وَتَعَالَىٰ says,

> "Let there be no shameful actions, bad deeds and fighting."*(Al–Baqarah* 2:197)

During the *Ḥajj,* a pilgrim visits *Bait–Allāh* in Makkah

and goes to *Minā, 'Arafāt* and *Muzdalifah.* Most *ḥujjāj* visit Madīnah before before or after the *Ḥajj. They offer the Ṣalāh* in the *Masjid an -Nabī.* They send *Salām* to *Rasūlullāh* ﷺ

A male pilgrim who makes the *Ḥajj* is called *al- Ḥajj.* A female pigrim who makes *Ḥajj* is called *al- Ḥajjah.* Allah ﷻ forgives all previous sins of those who perform the *Ḥajj.*

A New Birth

Rasūlullāh ﷺ said:

"Whoever visits *Bait-Allāh* and does not do bad deeds, he returns as pure as the new born baby."

(Muslim)

WE HAVE LEARNED:

* Every Muslim, if he can afford to, must perform the *Ḥajj* once in his life.
* During the *Ḥajj* a pilgrim visits *Bait–Allāh, Minā, 'Arafāt* and *Muzdalifah.*
* While on *Ḥajj* a pilgrim loves to visit *Masjid an–Nabī* for the *Ṣalāh,* and the grave of Rasūlullāh ﷺ to offer the Salām.

DO WE KNOW THESE WORDS?

Al–Ḥājj
Al–Ḥājjah
Bait–Allāh
Ḥajj
'iḥrām
respond

بِسْمِ اللهِ الرَّحْمٰنِ الرَّحِيْمِ

Lesson 2

بِسْمِ	In the name	اللهِ	*of Allah*
الرَّحْمٰنِ	the Mercy-Giving	الرَّحِيمِ	the Merciful

Lesson 3

اقْرَأْ	Read	بِاسْمِ	In the name of
رَبِّكَ	your Lord	الَّذِى	Who, He Who
خَلَقَ	created (you)		

Lesson 4

إِنَّ	Surely, verily	الدِّينَ	the (True) Religion
عِندَ	with	اللهِ	Allah
الإِسْلٰمُ	is Islam		

Lesson 5

ذٰلِكَ	This	الْكِتٰبُ	The Book
لاَ رَيْبَ	there is no doubt	فِيهِ	about it, in it
هُدًى	(it is) guidance	لِّلْمُتَّقِينَ	unto those who are Righteous, God-Conscious

Lesson 6

وَلَقَدْ	And indeed	يَسَّرْنَا	We have made easy
الْقُرآنَ	the Qur'an	لِلذِّكْرِ	for remembrance
فَهَلْ	but, is there any...?	مِن مُّدَّكِرٍ	person to do so (to heed remembrance)

Lesson 7

فَٱقْرَءُوا	therefore read	مَا تَيَسَّرَ	as mush as is easy
مِنَ	of , from	ٱلْقُرْآنِ	The Qur'an

Lesson 8

وَرَتِّلِ	And recite	ٱلْقُرْآنَ	the Qur'an
تَرْتِيلاً	in *Tartil* (slow measured tones)		

Lesson 10

وَإِنْ	And if	تَعُدُّوا	you would count
نِعْمَتَ	the blessings of	ٱللَّهِ	Allah
لاَ تُحْصُوهَآ	you cannot count them		

Lesson 11

وَمَا تَشَآءُونَ	And you do not will	إِلاَّ	unless
أَن يَشَآءَ ٱللَّهُ	Allah Wills	رَبُّ ٱلْعَٰلَمِينَ	the Lord of the Worlds

Lesson 12

إِنْ	If	يَنْصُرْكُمُ	helps you
ٱللَّهُ	Allah	فَلاَ غَالِبَ	no one can defeat
لَكُمْ	you	وَإِنْ	And if
يَخْذُلْكُمْ	He does not help you, He abandons you	فَمَنْ ذَا ٱلَّذِى	who is there
يَنصُرُكُم	that can help you	مِّن بَعْدِهِ	after that

Lesson 13

وَنَحْنُ	And We (Allah	أَقْرَبُ	are nearer
إِلَيْهِ	to him	مِنْ	than
حَبْلِ	vein (of)	ٱلْوَرِيدِ	jugular

Lesson 14

وَمَنْ	Whoever	يُشْرِكْ	accets partners
بِٱللَّهِ	with Allah	فَقَدْ	indeed
افْتَرَى	he has invented	إِثْمًا	sin
عَظِيمًا	a great		

Lesson 15

إِنَّ	Surly, indeed	شَرَّ	the worst (of)
الدَّوَآبِّ	the beasts	عِندَ ٱللَّهِ	in the Sight of Allah
ٱلَّذِينَ	(are) those who	كَفَرُوا	disbelieve
فَهُمْ	indeed they	لاَ يُؤْمِنُونَ	will not believe

Lesson 16

وَلَقَدْ	And indeed	بَعَثْنَا	We (Allah) have sent
فِي كُلِّ أُمَّةٍ	to every comunity	رَّسُولاً	a messenger
أَنِ ٱعْبُدُوا	who taught to worship (of)	اللَّهَ	Allah
وَٱجْتَنِبُوا	and to reject, to avoid	الطَّٰغُوتَ	the Evil

Lesson 17

لَقَدْ	Indeed	كَانَ لَكُمْ	you have
فِي	In	رَسُولِ ٱللَّهِ	the Messenger of Allah
أُسْوَةٌ	example	حَسَنَةٌ	a good

Lesson 18

قُلْ	Say	إِنْ كُنْتُمْ	If you
تُحِبُّونَ ٱللَّهَ	love Allah	فَٱتَّبِعُونِى	then follow me
يُحْبِبْكُمُ ٱللَّهُ	Allah will love you	وَيَغْفِرْ لَكُم	and forgive for you
ذُنُوبَكُمْ	your sins		

Lesson 19

اَلنَّبِيُّ	The Prophet	أَوْلَىٰ	is closer, more deserving (of love)
بِٱلْمُؤْمِنِينَ	to the Believers	مِنْ أَنفُسِهِمْ	than their own selves
وَأَزْوَٰجُهُ	and his wives	أُمَّهَـٰتُهُمْ	are their mothers

Lesson 20

جَآءَتْهُمْ	came to them	رُسُلُهُم	Their messengers
بِٱلْبَيِّنَـٰتِ	with clear proofs	وَبِٱلزُّبُرِ	and with *Zubur* (sacred books)
وَبِٱلْكِتَـٰبِ	and the Book	اَلْمُنِيرِ	giving light which gives light of (guidance)

Lesson 21

اَلْحَمْدُ لِلَّهِ	Praise be to Allah	فَاطِرِ	the Creator of
اَلسَّمٰوٰتِ	the heavens	وَٱلْأَرْضِ	and the earth
جَاعِلِ	who made	اَلْمَلٰٓئِكَةِ	the Angels
رُسُلاً	Messengers		

Lesson 22

وَلَدَارُ	And the house, the abode	اَلْأٰخِرَةِ	the Hereafter
خَيْرٌ	will be better	وَلَنِعْمَ	Pleasant indeed
دَارُ	the home of	اَلْمُتَّقِينَ	the righteous

Lesson 24

فَٱعْلَمْ	So, know	أَنَّهُ	that Indeed
لَا إِلٰهَ	that there is no god	إِلاَّ	except
ٱللَّهُ	Allah, the One God		

Lesson 25

مُحَمَّدٌ	Muhammad (is)	رَّسُولُ	the Messenger (of)
اَللَّهِ	Allah		

Lesson 26

وَأْمُرْ	And enjoin	أَهْلَكَ	upon your family
بِٱلصَّلٰوةِ	the *Salah*, the prayer	وَٱصْطَبِرْ	and be regular
عَلَيْهَا	in it		

Lesson 27

يَأَيُّهَا ٱلَّذِينَ ءَامَنُوا	O Believers	كُتِبَ	is made obligatory
عَلَيْكُمُ	for you	الصِّيَامُ	the *siyam*, the fasting
كَمَا	as it	كُتِبَ	was made obligatory
عَلَى ٱلَّذِينَ	upon those who	مِن قَبْلِكُمْ	before you
لَعَلَّكُمْ	that you may	تَتَّقُونَ	learn *taqwa,* consciousness of Allah

Lesson 28

فَأَقِيمُوا	So offer	الصَّلَوٰةَ	the *Salah,* prayer
وَءَاتُوا	and pay	الزَّكَوٰةَ	the *Zakah,* poor dues
وَٱعْتَصِمُوا	and hold fast	بِٱللَّهِ	to Allah
هُوَ	He is	مَوْلَىٰكُمْ	your Master

Lesson 29

وَلِلَّهِ	to Allah	عَلَى ٱلنَّاسِ	is a duty upon people
حِجُّ	to perform *Hajj* (pilgrimage)	الْبَيْتِ	to the House
مَنِ ٱسْتَطَاعَ	who can afford	إِلَيْهِ	to it
سَبِيلاً	a way, a path		

بِسۡمِ اللّٰهِ الرَّحۡمٰنِ الرَّحِيۡمِ

Glossary of Words

A

abuse: (v.) to treat badly, to harm; (v.) to use improperly; in excess; (n.) cruel treatment. e.g., The Prophet ﷺ suffered much abuse from the *Kuffār*.

accept: (v.) to receive with favor, to include. e.g., True Muslims accept the teachings of Islam.

accursed: (adj.) rejected, hated. e.g., The Shaitan is accursed by Allah.

Adam: (pr. n.) The first man and first messenger (*Rasūl*) of Allah.

***'adhān*:** (n.) the call for prayer.

afford: (v.) to be able to do something (v.) to have enough money to buy something or do something. e.g. Those who can afford to go for *Ḥajj* must do so.

***'ahādīth*:** (see *hadīth*)

***Al-'Ākhirah*:** (pr. n.) the other life, the final life after this one.

***'Alaihi (a)s-Salām*:** (ph.) "On him be peace." We say this to ask Allah's blessings, on the prophets and angels of Allah.

***Al-Basīr*:** The All-Seeing. One of the beautiful names of Allah.

Al-Bukhārīi: (pr. n.) Al-Bukhar:, full name Abu Abdullah Muhammad ibn Isma'il, (810-870CE). The author of a *hadīth* book Sahih Al-Bukhāri, named after him, which is considered the most reliable of the *hadīth* books.

***al-ḥājj*:** (adj.) a title of a man or boy who has performed the *Ḥajj*.

***al-ḥājjah*:** (adj.) a title of a woman or girl who has performed the *Ḥajj*.

***Alḥamdu li-(A)llāh*:** (ph.) "All praise is for Allah." First words of *Surat al-Fatihah*. We say this when we realize Allah's power and goodness.

***'ālim*:** (n.) "knower," the knowledgeable, a Muslim scholar.

angel: (n.) creatures made of light, made to obey Allah perfectly.

appreciate: (v) to understand the importance of something. e.g., When we become sick, we appreciate health.

***'Arkān*:** (pl. n. sing: *rukn*) "support", "basis"; the Arabic term for the pillars of Islam.The five *arkān* of Islam are: *Shahādah, Ṣalāh, Ṣawm, Ẓakāh,* and *Ḥajj*.

***'aslama*:** (v.) "to obey, to become a Muslim" *Aslama* is the root from which comes the word *Islam.*

astray: (adj.) off the right path, lost. e.g., Those who do bad things have gone astray.

'Āyah: a Sign of Allah, a single verse of the Qur'an.

B

***Bait-Ullāh*:** (pr.n,.) "House of Allah," the Ka'bah, or a mosque.

***barakah*:** (n.) blessing. e.g., Every good deed brings *barakah.*

benefit: (n.) a favor, a goodness, an advantage.

blessing: favor, reward, *barakah.*

C

Children of Adam: all human beings.

charity: (n.) doing good to others; money, food, clothes, and other items we give to the poor, needy, and for a good cause.

clot: (n.) very small lump, concreted blood. e.g., Humans are created from a clot of blood.

command: (v.) to order; (n.) an order. e.g., Allah commands us to do good.

create: (v.) to make, to form out of nothing.

D

Dāwūd: (pr.n.) a prophet of Islam. *Zabūr* was revealed to him.

defeat: (v.) to make your opponent lose. (n.) loss of a game, race or battle. e.g., In the Battle of Badr, the Muslims defeated their enemies.

develop: (v.) to grow, to change; to help something else grow, to mold.

discriminate: (v.) to note the differences between groups or ideas, to prefer one over other. e.g., We should not discriminate among people on the basis of their color or race.

***dunyā, ad-dunyā*:** (n.) this world, this life.

duty: (n.) responsibility, service.

E

enjoin: (v.) to order to do something, encourage.

F

***farḍ*:** (adj.) obligatory, an order, absolutely necessary.

favor: (n.) benefit, special reward, or help.
final: (adj.) last, the end, in a row.
forbid: (v.) to order not to do something
forgive: (v.) to stop being angry at a person for something he said or did.

G

generous: (adj.) giving; e.g., A generous person shares with others whatever Allah has given him.
guide: (v.) to show, instruct, or teach, to lead.

H

***ḥadīth*:** (n.) saying or happening. Reports about the sayings and actions of Rasūlullāh ﷺ. The *ḥadith* literature is a written collection of Rasūlullāh's sayings and actions.
***ḥāfiz*:** (n.plur: *ḥuffāz*) protector, someone who has memorized the entire Qur'an. e.g., The entire Qur'an is kept safe in the memory of a *ḥāfiz*.
***Ḥajj*:** (pr.n.) the pilgrimage (religious visit) to Makkah which all Muslims must try to make at least once in their lives.
***ḥakīm*:** (adj.) wise. Allah is *Al-Ḥakīm*, the All-Wise.
healthy: (adj.) something which is good for us; (adj.) someone who is strong and does not get sick easily.
Ḥirā': (pr. n) a cave near Makkah, where Rasūlullāh ﷺ would go to meditate before he became a prophet and received his first revelation *Waḥī*.
human: (n.) a person; men and women created by Allah.

I

***'ibādah*:** (n.) an act of worship.
'Ibrāhīm: (pr. n.) Abraham, prophet of Allah who with his son Ismā'il built the Ka'bah. He is the ancestor of Musā ﷺ, 'Īsā ﷺ and Muhammad ﷺ. *Suhuf* were revealed to him.
idol: (n.) statue or figure worshipped by some people.
ignorant: (adj.) without knowledge or understanding.
***'iḥrām*:** (n.) the white two-piece garment men wear on *Hajj*. For women, *iḥrām* is their regular Islamic dress.
***'imām*:** (n.) the leader of a Muslim community, leader of the *jamā'ah* of *Salāh*.
***'īmān*:** (n.) belief, faith in Allah and His Revelations.
***'Injīl*:** (pr. n. plur: *Anajīl*) the Gospels, books revealed to Prophet' *Īsa* ﷺ.

Innā li-(A)llāhi wa innā 'ilaihi raji'ūn : (ph.) "Indeed, we belong to Allah and to Him is our return." We say this when we hear of someone's death or personal loss.

Inshā'Allah: (ph.) "If Allah Wills." We say this whenever we speak of doing something in the future.

invent: (v.) to make something which no one has made before.

'iqāmah: (n.) "rising", a call to stand for the *jamā'ah.*

'Īsā: (n) Jesus son of Mary, a prophet of Allah. *Injīls* (Gospels) were revealed to him.

Isrāfil: (pr. n.) the angel who will blow the trumpet, *As-Sūr,* to announce the beginning of the Day of Judgement.

'Izrā'īl: (pr. n.) the angel of death, who removes souls from our bodies.

J

Jahannam: (pr. n.) hell, fire.

jamā'ah (n.) gathering, congregation, gathering to pray with others behind an *'imām.*

Jannah: (pr.n.) paradise, heaven.

Jibrīl: (pr. n.) the angel who delivered Allah's revelations (*Waḥī*) to the prophets.

jinn: (n.) creatures of fire whom we cannot see. Jinns, like humans, can choose to obey or disobey Allah ﷻ.

judge: (v.) to decide if an action is right or wrong; (n.) a person who makes such decisions. Allah ﷻ wants us to <u>judge</u> among people justly.

jugular vein: (n.) The most vital vein in our bodies. It runs along the left side of the neck to the heart.

juz': (n. plur: *ajza'*) part, one part of the Qur'an. The Qur'an has 30 *ajzā'.*

K

Kāfir: (n. plur: *kuffār*) an ungrateful person, a non-believer.

Kufr: (n.) ungratefulness, disbelief in Allah and in the judgment to come.

Kuffār: (pl. n. sing: *kāfir*) see *kāfir.*

M

malā'ikah: (pl. n. sing: *malak*) see *malak.*

malak: (n. plur: *malā'ikah*) angel, creature of light, made by Allah to obey Him. The *malā'ikah* cannot choose whether or not to obey Allah.

***Mā shā'Allah*:** (ph.) "Whatever Allah Wills." We say this when we hear of something good, when we appreciate something.

***masjid*:** (n. plur: *masājid)* "place of *sajdah*," a place of *ṣalāh*, a mosque.

***Masjid an-Nabī*:** The mosque of the Prophet ﷺ in Madinah.

measured: (adj) counted slow, rhythmic, thoughtful.

memorize: (v.) to learn something by heart. e.g., *Ḥuffāz* memorize the entire Qur'an and recite it without seeing it.

mercy: (n.) kindness, forgiveness.

***Mikā'īl*:** (pr. n.) the angel who oversees the amount of rain we receive.

Minā: (pr. n.) a place near Makkah, one of the places visited by pilgrims during *Ḥajj*.

model: (n.) an example to follow; (v.) to imitate. e.g., Rasūlullāh ﷺ is the best model for us.

moral: (n.) rules, regulations and teaching about how to be a good person.

***mu'min*:** (n. plur: *mu'minūn*) A Believer, another term for a Muslim.

***munafiqūn*:** (pl. n. sing: *munāfiq*) "hypocrites," a group of people at the time of the Prophet ﷺ who pretended to believe but in fact did not.

***muqrī*:** (n.) "a reader, a reciter" a person who knows how to read the Qur'an beautifully. One who knows *tajwīd* and *tartīl*. Same as *qārī'*.

***Mūsā*:** Moses, a prophet of Islam, *Tawrait* (Torah was revealed to him).

***mushrikūn*:** (pl. n. sing: *mushrīk*) "people who do *shirk*," people who believe that Allah shares His power with others.

Muslim: (n.) Literally, one who submits to Allah, one who follows Islam. (Pr.n.) Abu al-Husain 'Asakir ad-Dīn ibn Hajjāj (817-874CE) author of the second most reliable of the *ḥadīth* books *Sahīh Muslim* named after him.

muttaqīn: (pl. n. sing: *muttaqi*) "those who have *taqwa*." People who fear Allah and follow His laws exactly. The Righteous.

Muzdalifah: (pr. n.) one of the places visited by pilgrims during *Ḥajj*.

N

***nabī*:** (n.) prophet.

O

obey: (v.) to follow orders. e.g. We must obey Allah and His Messengers.

obligatory: (adj.) necessary, must be done, *fard*. e.g., *Ṣalāh* is obligatory on every Muslim.

P

patience: (n.) the willingness to wait for others, to suffer without complaining. The Arabic word for patience is *ṣabr.*

permission: (n.) approval. e.g., The students must ask teacher's permission before they can leave the classroom.

permit: (v.) to allow, give permission. Islam does not permit us to steal or to use bad language.

pilgrimage: (n.) a religious visit to some sacred place, *Ḥajj.*

pillar: (n.) a support for a building. The pillars of Islam, the *arkān.*

pleasant: (adj.) nice, pleasing, restful.

purify: (v.) to clean, to get rid of all elements which do not belong. e.g., We must purify our thoughts from bad ideas.

Q

***qārī'*:** (n.) One who reads the Qur'an beautifully. see also *muqrī.*

***qawī*:** (adj.) "powerful." Allah is *Al-Qawi*, the All-Powerful.

Qadar: (n.) Allah's decree; His Power and knowledge of whatever is written for each human soul.

R

***Raḥīm*:** (adj.) "compassionate." Allah refers to Himself as *Ar-Raḥīm* in the Qur'an.

***Raḥmān*:** (adj.) "merciful." Allah also refers to Himself as *Ar-Raḥmān*, the All-Merciful, in the Qur'an.

***rasūl*:** (n. plur: *rusul)* "messenger", someone sent with a *Waḥī*, with a specific message from Allah in the form of a book. Prophets *'Īsā, Mūsā, Dāwūd, 'Ibrāhīm*, and *Muḥammad* ﷺ were *rusul.*

***Rasūlullāh*:** (n.) "Messenger of Allah." We call Prophet Muhammad ﷺ *Rasūlullāh.*

recite: (v.) to read something out loud, or to say it clearly, with rhythm. Some things which are recited are the Qur'an and poetry.

refuge: (n.) safety, security, a safe place.

regular: (adj.) 1. even, smooth. 2. on time, on schedule.

reject: (v.) to deny, to exclude. "To reject" is the opposite of "to accept."

relative: (n.) someone who is in your family.

repent: (v.) to regret, to feel sorry, to ask for forgiveness. e.g., For all our mistakes, we must repent to Allah.

reveal: (v.) to make known, allow to be seen, inspiration by God. e.g., The Qur'an was revealed to Prophet Muhammad ﷺ by Allah ﷻ.
righteous: (adj.) one who tries to do things rightly, moral, correct.

S

***ṣabr*:** (n.) patience, not showing anger in difficulties, accepting whatever happens with faith in Allah.
sacrifice: (v.) to offer something to God; to give something away dear to you for some person or cause.
***ṣadaqah*:** (n.) charity, anything we give beyond the *Ẓakāh*.
safeguard: (v.) to protect, keep safe: (n.) protection.
***Ṣaḥābah*:** (pl. n. sing: *Ṣaḥābi*) companions of Rasūlullāh ﷺ.
***Ṣalāh*:** (n.) the formal prayer which Muslims must do five times a day.
***salām*:** (n.) peace, Islamic greeting *as-Salām*, The Peace, is one of God's names.
Salātu 'ala-(a)n-Nabī: (n.) [also called darūd in Persian/urdu]: salutations on the Messenger ﷺ.
***salima*:** (v.) "to be at peace." *Salima* is related to the word "Islam."
***Ṣall(a) Allāhu`alai-hi wa Ṣallam*:** (ph.) "Peace of Allah and His blessings be upon him." This is how we ask Allah's peace upon the Prophet ﷺ.
salutation: (n.) greeting, wishing well, welcoming.
***Ṣawm*:** (n.) fasting, fasting during the month of Ramadan, same as *siyām*.
scripture: (n.) a written revelation, or a sacred book of religion.
seal: (n.) a closing mark, such as a seal on an envelope. Muhammad ﷺ is the seal of Prophets.
***Shahādah*:** (n.) to bear witness, part of Islamic faith to bear witness that Allah is.
***Shaitān*:** (pr. n.) Satan, the Devil, the enemy of all human beings.
shameful: (adj.) full of shame, disgrace, wrong, embarrassment.
***Shirk*:** (n.) accepting partners with Allah, making other things equal to Allah.
***Ṣihāh Sittāh*:** (pr. n.) the six most important books of '*aḥādīth*.
sin: (n.) a bad deed; (v.) to do something bad, unjust, forbidden e.g., *Shirk* is the worst sin in Islam.
***siyām*:** (n.) fasting, see also *ṣawm*.
***Subhān(a) Allāh*:** (ph.) "Glorified is Allah." We say this when we see some thing beautiful or appreciate something.
***Ṣuḥuf*:** (pr. n.) the scriptures revealed to Prophet *Ibrāhīm* عليه السلام
***Sunnah*:** (n.) the life and practices of Rasūlullāh ﷺ.
support: (v.) to help someone; to comfort; to care for; someone or something.

e.g., The pillars support a building.

***Ṣūr*:** (pr. n.) a trumpet which will be blown by Angel *Israfil* at the beginning of the Day of Judgment.

***Sūrah*:** (n.) chapter of the Qur'ān. *Suwar* are revealed in various lengths. The Qur'an has 114 *Suwar*.

surrender: (v.) to give up totally, to submit. e.g., A Muslim, is one who surrenders himself to Allah ﷻ.

T

***tajwīd*:** (n.) a way of reading the Qur'an in slow rhythm.

***taqwa*:** (n.) love, fear, and awareness of Allah, purity of faith.

***tartīl*:** (n.) a way of reading the Qur'an in a faster rhythm.

***tawbah*:** (n.) "turning", repentance, turning to Allah for forgiveness.

***Tawḥīd*:** (n.) the Oneness of Allah. Allah has no partners and no parts.

***Tawrait*:** (pr. n.) the Torah, revealed to Prophet *Musā* ﷺ.

trust: (n.) the confidence, belief in someone to be honest.
(v.) to have faith, to believe.

U

***'ummah*:** (n.) community, or nation, group of people who have something in common. e.g., Muslims are one *'ummah* because of their common faith.

***Ummāhat ul-Mu'minīn*:** (pl. n. sing: *umm*) "mothers," title of Prophets' wives.

V

vein: (n.) one of two kinds of blood vessels. Veins are like long tubes that carry dirty blood to the heart to be cleaned.

vessel: (n.) container, blood vessels which contain and carry blood.

W

***Waḥī*:** (n.) revelation from Allah ﷻ to one of His prophets.

wealth: (n.) riches, prosperity, well-being.

will: (n.) intention; (v.) to intend. e.g., Where there is a will, there is a way.

womb: (n.) the place where the baby develops in the body of his mother.

worship: (v.) to pray, to serve.

Z

Zabūr: (pr. n.) Psalms, book revealed to Prophet *Dāwūd* ﷺ.

Zakāh: (n.) "purification" the practice of giving some of our savings to needy Muslims.

INTRODUCING THE AUTHORS

Dr. Abidullah Ghazi, Executive Director of IQRA' International, and his wife, Dr. Tasneema Ghazi, Director of Curriculum, are co–founders of IQRA' International Educational Foundation (a non–profit Islamic educational trust established in 1983) and Chief Editors of its educational program. They have combined their talents and expertise and, for the last two decades, dedicated their lives to produce a Comprehensive Program of Islamic Studies for our children and youth and to develop IQRA' into a major center of research and development for Islamic Studies, specializing in Islamic education.

Abidullah Ghazi, M. A. (Alig), M. Sc. Econ. (LSE London), Ph. D. (Harvard)

Dr. Abidullah Ghazi, a specialist in Islamic Studies and Comparative Religion, belongs to a prominent family of the Ulama' of India. His family has been active in the field of Islamic education, *dawah*, and struggle for freedom. Dr. Ghazi's early education was carried in traditional *Madāris*. He has studied at Muslim University, Aligarh, The London School of Economics, and Harvard University. He has taught at the Universities of Jamia Millia Islamia, Delhi, London, Harvard, San Diego, Minnesota, Northwestern, Governors State and King Abdul Aziz (Jeddah). He is a consultant for the development of the program of Islamic Studies in various schools and universities. He is a well–known community worker, speaker, writer and poet.

Tasneema K. Ghazi, M. A. (Alig), M. Ed. (Allahabad), Acd. Dip. (London), CAGS (Harvard), Ph. D. (Minnesota)

Dr. Tasneema Ghazi is a specialist in Child Development and Reading (Curriculum and Instruction). She has studied at the Universities of Aligarh, Allahabad, London, Harvard, San Diego, and Minnesota. She has taught in India, England, Saudi Arabia, and the United States at various levels: kindergarten, elementary, junior, senior and university. Since her arrival in the USA in 1968, she has been involved with the schools of Islamic Studies providing them valuable advice and guidance. Working with children is her main interest.

Dr. and Mrs. Ghazi have a life–long commitment to write, develop and produce Islamic educational material and quality textbooks at various levels. Dr. Tasneema Ghazi has completed Pre–school and Kindergarten Curricula and plans to produce an integrated curriculum from pre–school to high school by 1998, *Insha Allah*.

Their textbooks on the *Sīrah* and other Islamic subjects have become standard textbooks in Islamic schools in USA and all across the world, and are being published in several parts of the world and translated in major languages of the world.

They have five children, Bushra, Rashid, Saba' and twins, Suhaib and Usama. Their children provided them with their first experimental lab. They are also their co–workers.